KV-193-726

HOUSE PLANTS

HOW TO SELECT & CARE
FOR YOUR PLANTS

ORBIS · LONDON

Acknowledgments

A-Z Botanical Collection Limited 50, 65 (top),
86, 90; Michael Nicholson/Elizabeth Whiting
Associates (designer Maggi Henry) 15; Photos
Horticultural 11, 23, 24, 25, 27, 29, 51 (bottom),
89 (top), 91 (top); Harry Smith Horticultural
Photographs 77 (top); Spectrum Colour
Library 10-11, 28; Transworld Feature Syndicate
(Elyse Lewin) 13

All the remaining photographs in the book were
taken by Terry Long and Neil Wood

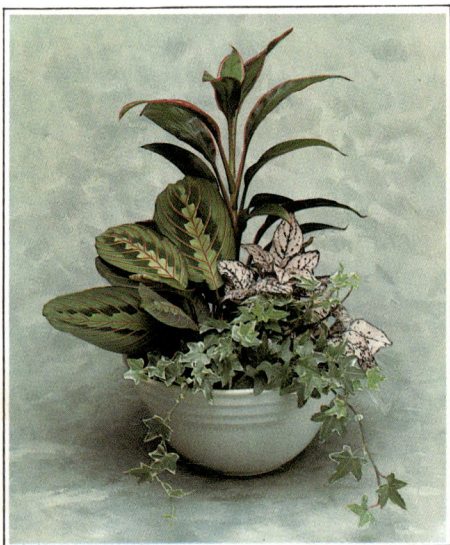

The publishers would like to thank The Geest
Organization, Clifton Nurseries Limited
and The Plant People Limited for supplying plants
for photography

First published in Great Britain by
Orbis Publishing Limited, London 1984 for
The Littlewoods Organization plc
Reprinted 1986 by Orbis Book Publishing Corporation Ltd.
A BPCC plc company

© 1984 Orbis Publishing Limited

All rights reserved. No part of this publication may
be reproduced, stored in a retrieval system, or
transmitted, in any form or by any means
electronic, mechanical, photocopying, recording or
otherwise, without the prior permission of the
publishers. Such permission, if granted, is subject
to a fee depending on the nature of the use.

Series Art Editor Grahame Dudley
Filmset by Peter MacDonald Typesetting,
Twickenham

Printed in Yugoslavia
ISBN 1-85155-056-9

CONTENTS

TYPES OF PLANTS

Growing indoor plants is an absorbing and rewarding interest. Through careful choice, any home can be turned into a haven of healthy foliage, summer and winter, or brightened with richly coloured flowers in the appropriate seasons. The increasing popularity of houseplants in recent years has meant that a greater range of plants has become widely available – tentative newcomers to indoor gardening can choose hardy, adaptable foliage plants and flowering annuals, while the more ambitious can expand their collections to include unusual items that need a little bit of extra care.

Green fingers can be acquired – most failures with houseplants are attributable to incorrect growing conditions and care. Attention to a few basic facts about the general needs and specific preferences of plants can quickly result in a flourishing display. A sunny, airy windowsill may be your idea of a perfect environment for houseplants, but it is not universally attractive to the plants themselves. There are those that prefer continuous cool temperatures or partial shade, others that must have sun while flowering but not during the winter rest. Even if in the past you have had disasters with houseplants, you can look forward to achieving

success by finding the types that are naturally suited to the care and conditions you can offer them.

There are three general categories of plants sold for indoor cultivation. Foliage houseplants are relatively long-lived and provide a good showing throughout the year. Some lead a quietly consistent life, while others have more pronounced seasonal cycles of active growth alternating with complete rest, but they do not shed their leaves like the deciduous plants outdoors.

Flowering plants fall into two basic types. Those which are properly described as houseplants will survive for a prolonged period indoors, flowering at the appropriate seasons in successive years, after periods of rest or dormancy when growth ceases and the foliage dies back temporarily. The category often described as flowering pot plants includes annuals – plants which complete their entire growth cycle within twelve months and have no further potential – and species which were originally garden plants and have been adapted for short-term life indoors. These are kept in the house for as long as they flower and can then be discarded or planted out in the garden. Bulbs such as Tulips, Crocuses and Narcissi can be transferred, and Primulas and Chrysanthemums

1 Begonia
2 Exacum affine
3 Kalanchoë blossfeldiana

may survive in an outdoor bed. Cyclamen and Poinsettia, with their vivid blooms and bracts, are often sold as 'gift plants' and are thrown away after a short period of splendour. It is possible to maintain these plants and persuade them to flower a following year, but they need special care and are something of a challenge, so don't be disappointed if they fail to reach a second season.

Every plant has a typical growth habit: the term refers to the overall shape of the plant, the direction of growth, and whether or not stems are self-supporting. Vertical plants may be like miniature trees – e.g. Yucca (p. 94) and Dracaena (p. 58) – or alternatively have tough fleshy leaves – tall spears like those of Sansevieria (p. 84) or broad, spreading leaves on a strong central stem, as in Ficus 'Robusta' (p. 62). There are grassy plants with elegantly arching leaves, of which the most popular is Chlorophytum, the Spider Plant. The category generally described as bushy plants includes a great many varieties, typically having multiple stems and spreading leaves. The plants may be foliage or flowering, green or variegated, soft, succulent or woody-stemmed. Climbing and trailing plants are much appreciated for a flamboyant display where space is limited, and these include tolerant specimens such as Tradescantia (p. 92) and Hedera (p. 66) and some more delicate flowering plants, including Jasmine (p. 72) and Passiflora

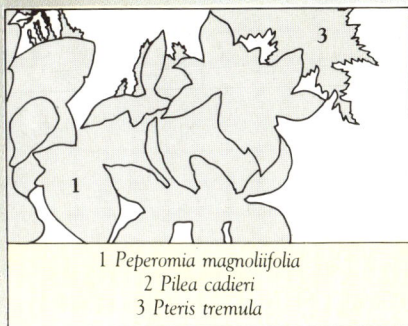

1 *Peperomia magnoliifolia*
2 *Pilea cadieri*
3 *Pteris tremula*

(p. 76). Saintpaulia (p. 84) and Primula (p. 81), with their brightly coloured flowers, are among the plants which grow in a compact rosette shape, as are exotic-looking bromeliads, with thick, striped leaves.

The Latin names of houseplants often seem complicated to the lay person, but it is worth getting to know them as they are an unambiguous classification. Common names are often shared by several plants; using the botanical (Latin) name will ensure that you get the right plant, and that you know how to give it proper care, as plants with the same generic name do not always have the same needs.

A plant's genus is identified in the first of its Latin names. In formal identification this is written with a capital initial letter and is followed by a specific name written entirely in small letters, usually but not invariably italics – e.g. *Monstera deliciosa*. Professional plant-growers also develop different varieties within the species. These are technically known as cultivars and are identified by a third name in the sequence; the cultivar may have different coloured leaves or flowers, for example, from those of the original plant. Hybrids are plants bred from two members of the same family; in general these combine and emphasize certain characteristics of the parent plants. The name of a hybrid includes the symbol '×' to indicate the cross-breeding.

Generic classification is based on features of the botanical structure of plants, as is the broader grouping of plants under family names. Different species within the same genus or family do not necessarily look alike, as the common characteristic may relate to internal structure or, for example, to whether the plant reproduces by seeds or spores.

Plants have developed their structure and appearance in response to their native conditions. Many houseplants originate from semi-tropical or tropical zones and would live naturally in jungles, forests or swamps, or perhaps come from scrubland or desert. They have accustomed themselves to particular conditions and can prove equally adaptable to living indoors, provided their basic needs are respected.

CHOOSING AND BUYING PLANTS

The first thing to note about buying a new plant is that it has been raised in a protected, highly controlled environment and will need time to adjust to conditions in your home. It may show no activity for several days, but do not rush to give it food, water and a different position every day. Give it time to settle in. Whatever the condition of the plant, it will need this period, but you can get off to a good start by making sure you buy a healthy plant: protect it while travelling, however briefly, and offer it a situation which as far as possible caters to its basic needs and special requirements.

Be realistic about the amount of time you can spend on caring for plants. If you simply want a green corner to cheer up the room, choose foliage plants that can tolerate occasional neglect, not those which must constantly have their compost checked, falling leaves removed or growth trimmed and trained. If you would like to treat plants as a major hobby, then work out groupings of plants with similar requirements, look for fast-growers that need varied seasonal care and annual repotting, and choose trailers and climbers that can be put in baskets or arranged to enhance the appearance of the room.

If you are planning to keep plants as a decorative feature in a particular room, or you have only one or two places – windowsill or alcove – where plants can be accommodated, then make a note of the level of light and temperature in that space and take measurements. Thermometers and humidity gauges are not necessary: simply make a comparison of different rooms, or parts of a room, and assess the conditions on a scale of cold, cool, warm or hot and a range from full light, through poor light, to full shade. The amount of space is important – most plants are quite young when sold and some may be expected to spread or gain height considerably in a relatively short time. Look through the A-Z of plants starting on page 36, and match their features and requirements to conditions in your home.

If you are given to impulse buying, check the plant tag, which shows its preferences, to avoid making unnecessary mistakes. Don't buy a shade-loving plant if you live in a sunny bedsitter, or flowers needing warmth and sun if your house is draughty and dimly lit. Consider also how the plant will look in its new position. Pale walls and large windows show off many types of plants; dark walls reflect no extra light for the plant's benefit and may mask its shape, so choose striking outlines or pale foliage colours.

Buy plants from retail premises that are adequately lighted and reasonably warm. Choose a crisp specimen with unblemished leaves and clean growing tips. Check under the leaves for signs of insect attack. Reputable suppliers take care to keep their plants pest-free, but an infested plant is not only in danger itself – it

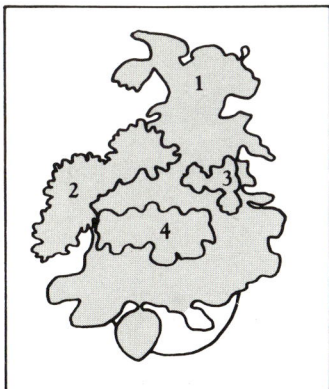

1 *Hedera canariensis*
2 *Chrysanthemum*
3 *Begonia semperflorens*
4 *Saintpaulia*

For a mixed display of flowering and foliage plants grouped in the same container, buy plants which will tolerate similar conditions. Saintpaulia, the African Violet, is the most demanding of the plants in this arrangement. The others are tolerant species and should succeed in most conditions, including those imposed on them by the Saintpaulia.

will pass the problem on to other plants in your home. Touch the compost to find out whether it is moist or dry. If the potting mixture has shrunk away from the sides of the pot, then the plant is underwatered and may have suffered. If compost is dry but the plant looks healthy except for a slight limpness, it can probably be revived by correct watering when you get it home. If a plant is wilting because the compost is waterlogged, there may well be severe root damage that cannot be cured. Don't make it your mission to rescue damaged plants – you are bound to have a very high failure rate.

Houseplants in an outdoor display must be tolerant of changing temperatures. Be wary of stall or pavement displays that include unfamiliar plants or those that you know to be temperamental. Choose garden flowering plants, or hardy foliage types.

When carrying a plant home, try to protect it from being bruised or crushed and avoid extremes of temperature. If transporting a plant in cold weather, wrap it well in paper and return home as soon as possible. In hot weather, do not leave a plant in a closed car, where it may be suffocated or scorched. In general, if you buy plants while doing other shopping, make the plants the last item you buy.

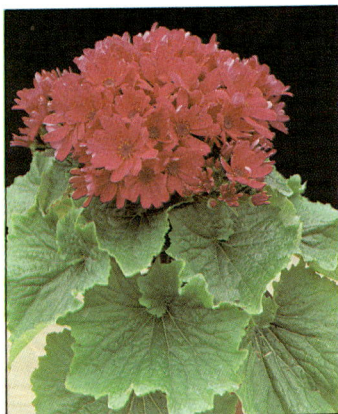

The growth habits of some plants make them particularly striking when displayed as solitary specimens in thoughtfully chosen situations. Above: the bright flowers and coarse green foliage of this Cineraria look handsome against a dark background.

Left: Nephrolepis bostoniensis is a magnificent plant for a large bright window, where its delicate foliage will appear in silhouette during the day.

Make sure the plant seems to have the correct growth habit and is neither swamped by its pot nor bursting out of it. Choose flowering plants that are in bud but just about to bloom. Tight flower buds may never open in conditions at home, but plants with full-blown flowers are already past their prime.

Some houseplants have been tended in the nursery for a few years before they are put on sale. Large, showy plants, such as palms, ferns and species with broad, glossy leaves will be expensive, but they are long-lived and have had good cultivation while becoming established.

Palms should be about 25cm (10in) high when you buy them. Younger palms, though cheaper, are still vulnerable and will be less likely to adapt to new conditions. Fast-growing and short-lived plants are often inexpensive, though gift plants with exotic blooms may be relatively costly if discarded after the short but spectacular flowering period. Small flowering plants are cheap and cheerful, whether they are annuals or live on to another growing season. Many foliage plants are very good value when bought young – tolerant trailing and bushy plants expand rapidly during their active growth periods and will flourish for months and years afterwards.

WHAT GOES WHERE

Plants enliven a room and you will want to place them where they look most attractive and can be seen and appreciated much of the time. They should also be within easy reach for watering and tending. But houseplants have preferences about where they live, and to avoid disappointment over a poor show of flowers or limp, chilled foliage, you must primarily take the plant's needs into consideration. Many plants will adapt to less than ideal conditions and several species are naturally suited to difficult places – a shady corner or cool north-facing window with little light – but others demand a much more comfortable environment.

Light and temperature are the most crucial factors – humidity can be controlled, though if you want to keep plants in the kitchen or bathroom, they must obviously be types that can stand a moist atmosphere. Avoid extreme conditions. Plants in a sunny window suffer leaf scorching if pressed to the glass under direct, hot sun, and the compost will dry out more quickly. Extreme cold is detrimental to all houseplants and even adaptable plants will object to continual fluctuations in temperature or frequent cold draughts from doors and windows.

One basic rule is that green foliage plants survive much better than flowering plants in poor light, and variegated foliage needs some good light to maintain its colours. The vivid blooms of Impatiens, Primulas and Pelargoniums are a happy choice for a bright, sunny windowsill; the red and yellow foliage of Codiaeum or cool green and cream of Chlorophytum benefit from a position near a window; further into the room where light is dim, you can keep a plant with large leaves adapted to making the most of available light, such as Monstera deliciosa or Ficus 'Robusta'. A south-facing window gets the most sun, but do not assume all light-loving plants must look south. Many appreciate the less fierce rays of morning or afternoon sun and may prefer a window facing east or west. Green plants do well in north light with no sun, but there is no need to restrict the choice entirely to these. Bulbs, Dianthus or Chrysanthemums can provide seasonal colour in a north-facing window, or choose the spectacular Columnea, a trailing plant with a heavy cascade of dark foliage and bright orange-red flowers.

Plants are most often kept in the living room or kitchen. These frequently used rooms tend to have the best light and regular temperatures. The plants' progress is constantly on view, so it is worth trying more delicate varieties in the living room, as well as the large range of tolerant and adaptable plants. Central heating has a drying effect, so you should make sure the plants have enough moisture (see p. 22). Do not place or hang plants directly over a source of heat – above a radiator or by the cooker. Fleshy,

Ferns are a natural choice for bathrooms, as they thrive in moist conditions. Even so, fluctuating temperatures and humidity levels should be avoided when possible.

glossy leaves have the greatest tolerance of a stuffy atmosphere and of fumes from cooking or heating appliances.

Other parts of the house may be unheated except when actually in use. Bedrooms and a dining or sitting room apart from the main living room may be relatively cool most of the time. There are some lovely flowering plants that enjoy cool temperatures – Cyclamen, Hydrangea and Campanula – or you can choose a tiny-leaved Helxine, purple-tinted Gynura, or more flamboyant foliage plant such as Cissus or Rhoicissus.

Ferns are the great standby for difficult areas – a room with permanently poor light or the moist air of a bathroom. They are naturally adapted to these conditions. A bathroom with an even, relatively warm temperature can become a marvellous display of feathery, spiky and curling foliage. Asparagus is a good choice if you have space for a spreading plant, or choose the sturdier, more compact shape of Pellaea, the Button Fern.

Large foliage plants look well in the hall or on the landing, but these are the places where draughts are most frequently felt, and they may also be somewhat dark. Place hardy foliage plants out of the direct line from the front door. For a hanging plant on the stairwell, try Chlorophytum, Tradescantia or Hedera – tolerant plants with attractive leaf colours.

The choice between keeping a few single specimens or arranging massed groups of varied types depends upon your preference and the time you can give them. Plants grouped together must like or tolerate similar conditions. An interesting easy-care arrangement can be devised using green foliage interspersed with variegated plants. Combinations of flowering and foliage plants can be livened up seasonally if the plants are kept in separate pots and you can exchange, for example, a winter-flowering plant for one that blooms through spring and summer. Excellent effects are achieved either by grouping several plants of the same type in a dense cluster, or by introducing definite contrasts of height, colour, leaf shape and texture.

Window sills, ledges and alcoves are natural homes for plants. Be wary of low tabletops or surfaces constantly in use. A good idea for plants that need tender care is to keep the pots on a trolley with castors, so they can be easily wheeled away from hot sun or cold windows. Hanging baskets, suspended from hooks inserted in high ceilings, or above a window, are useful if space is limited. A window shelf, mounted about halfway up the frame, is a perfect showcase for trailing plants.

Large ferns and palms may grow to such a height that the container must be on or near floor level. As a general rule, small plants should be at or below eye level, trailers at or above eye level and large, showy plants arranged to minimize the effect of bare stems and draw attention to the spreading foliage above. Mask leggy plants by grouping smaller, bushy varieties around the base.

A few carefully chosen and well-placed plants can transform a room. Trailing species on a high shelf introduce a new level of interest, as do tall specimens such as this splendid Weeping Fig (Ficus benjamina) standing by the window.

Note that ordinary light bulbs and spotlights generate a lot of heat and do not satisfy a plant's need for light. The only type of artificial light in the home that actually encourages growth is cool white or daylight fluorescent tubes. Even so, these must burn for several hours a day to support foliage growth. Highlight a group of plants after dark, for a dramatic effect, but use artificial light as a supplement to daylight, not as the only light source.

BULBS

A pot of fresh-flowering bulbs in winter or early spring gives a delightful preview of the new growing season to come. Crocuses, Hyacinths, Narcissi and Tulips are garden bulbs and have only a short life in the home. They are treated for indoor cultivation and can be forced into early flowering, but afterwards should be thrown away or saved for planting out in the garden.

Bulbs are easy to grow, but things can go wrong. The key to successful cultivation is to give the plants the right degree of warmth and light at each stage of growth. If you buy bulbs already potted, look for healthy shoots about 2·5 cm (1in) high; Hyacinths are often bought at a later stage, with flower buds developing.

While the plants have young shoots, keep them at a cool

temperature – around 10°C (50°F) – and in average light or partial shade. When the leaves have properly started the plants require good light, otherwise growth will be stringy and pale, and when flower buds show they prefer a slightly warmer environment of 15°C (60°F). High temperatures and dry heat will inhibit flowering and the plants will benefit from a cool position at night – this encourages longer flowering. Turn the pot frequently when it is in full light, so the growth is even and straight.

Keep the potting mixture moist but not wet. Since the plants are a short-term venture there is no need to feed them. Take care not to splash water on the flower buds while they are developing. If the plant is over- or under-watered the leaves will turn yellow.

You can pot up bulbs and Crocus corms in autumn, in September or October. If you buy bulbs specially treated for indoor growth they must be planted immediately. They can be grown in flower pots, or in bowls with no drainage holes, provided drainage is good within the pot. Place small pieces of charcoal in the bottom of the bowl. Bulbs can be potted in bulb fibre, a mixture of sphagnum moss, crushed charcoal and oyster shell. It is light and easily handled but must be thoroughly wetted and drained before planting. If you want to plant the bulbs on into the garden, pot them initially in a more nourishing loam-based potting mixture.

Layer in the bulb fibre and pack it round the bulbs, so their tips are level with the top of the pot. Place the pot in a cool, dark place or wrap it in a black polythene bag and put it in a cool room. When top shoots show, in five to eight weeks, bring the container to a position with subdued light and let the new shoots adjust for several days before they are exposed to full light. Keep them cool at first and warmer when flower buds appear.

To transfer the bulbs to the garden after flowering, wait until leaves have died right back, take the bulbs out of the pot and let them dry out. Plant them out the following autumn.

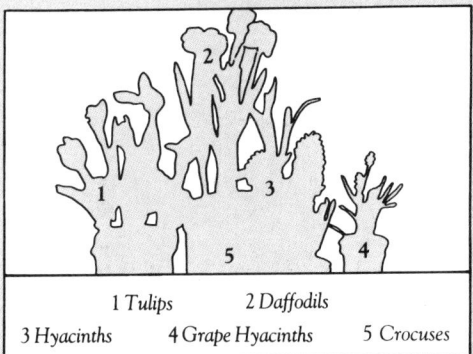

1 Tulips   2 Daffodils
3 Hyacinths   4 Grape Hyacinths   5 Crocuses

CACTI

Chamacereus

Gymnocalycium

Haworthia

Opuntia

Rebutia

Desert cacti are popular houseplants, attracting attention for their interesting shapes and tolerant natures. Being tolerant, they are often unfairly neglected. They can survive dramatic changes of temperature, poor soil and long periods of drought, but it should not be assumed that cacti actually enjoy these conditions. In fact, with proper care, many can be encouraged to become highly active plants that flower annually. Their own health is improved and they make a more attractive show.

Cacti require plenty of light, summer and winter, and flourish through warm summer days; but in winter they need a rest period and should be placed in a cool room, neither suffocated by central heating nor frozen near a cold window. Cacti need water as do all plants, but they can store it for quite long periods in their succulent stems. From April to August the compost should be kept continually moist with tepid water, though never saturated. Decrease watering gradually through autumn and leave the plants almost dry until the following March. Overwatering will cause stems to shrivel or to show brown, rotting patches. Lack of growth probably points to watering problems – too little in summer, too much in winter. Correct this and cut away rotted areas of stem.

Despite their origins, cacti kept indoors do not like to live in sand. A mixture of one part coarse sand to two parts loam-based compost has good drainage, preventing root rot, and supplies essential nutrients. During active growth the plants will appreciate an occasional feed, watered into the potting mixture.

Flowering in cacti depends upon new growth and may not occur until the plant's fourth or fifth year. The fleshy stems are covered with areoles – bristly pads with outgrowing spines, hooks or hairs. Each areole produces only one flower in the lifetime of the plant, so the cactus must grow bigger and develop new areoles to have a chance of further flowering. The blooms are usually bell- or trumpet-shaped; size and colour vary between different species.

Repot cacti annually while they are young, into a pot only one size larger. They benefit from being slightly pot-bound, so in later years potting on should be unnecessary. When handling the plant use a folded sheet of paper as a sling, wrapped gently around the stem. Tap the pot to loosen the soil; do not drag the cactus out of its container.

Mamillaria, Ferocactus and Lobivia are attractive ball-shaped plants; Chamacereus and Cleistocactus are finger cacti, and Opuntia develop curious multiple forms, with 'rabbit's ears' of new growth. Notocactus and Rebutia are popular forms that include both ball and finger species. These are all desert cacti; forest cacti are more flamboyant but they have different needs and require more care (see Schlumbergera and Zygocactus).

COMPOSTS AND CONTAINERS

Plastic pots are now the most common containers for houseplants. Clay pots are still available, but are often more difficult to find. The choice is entirely yours, as it makes no difference to the plants. Clay pots are heavy, providing balance for large plants, but they are porous, losing moisture through the sides, as well as from top and bottom, so more frequent watering is required. Plastic pots are clean, colourful and not liable to break easily.

Clay pots usually have only one drainage hole and must be crocked in the base with shards from a broken pot, whereas plastic pots have several holes and are free-draining. Typically, a pot is as deep as it is round. Pot sizes range in diameter from 4cm (1½in) to 38cm (15in). This measurement is made across the top of the pot, inside the rim. The usual sizes needed for most houseplants are from 7·5cm (3in) up to 25cm (10in).

If you want to place the plant in a decorative container – wood, metal or ceramic – with no drainage hole, it is best to stand the pot inside, rather than plant directly into the container. If you do pot up plants in a non-draining container, put a layer of gravel or charcoal in the base before adding the compost. Line a metal container with plastic, as some metals affect the roots of plants. You can use non-waterproof outer containers – baskets, for example – if they are lined with plastic or fitted with drip trays. Large tubs, troughs and trays are sold with and without drainage holes and can be used for planting, or to contain grouped pots.

Self-watering pots have a built-in reservoir and water gauge. This is convenient for holiday periods, but these pots are best used for large, showy specimens that need constant moisture. A multiple planter, like a small, recessed tower, is an attractive and unusual showcase for small foliage or flowering plants. Hanging baskets are popular for trailing plants. Mesh baskets must be lined with plastic hanging pots, which are also available separately. They are clean and convenient for watering and tending the plants, being lightweight and equipped with drip trays fixed in place. You can also find wall brackets of plastic-coated wire or metal, shaped to hold smaller pot sizes.

There are two basic types of potting mixture – soils, which are loam-based composts, and soil-less mixtures, largely consisting of peat. It is easy to tell which compost the plant is in when you buy it – peat composts are dark brown and crumbly, loamy soil is lighter in colour and more gritty. Peat-based composts are light and clean, but they dry out quickly and give less weight in the pot to balance a tall stem or spreading foliage. Proprietary brand composts are sterilized and contain special nutrients. Never pot plants in garden soil, as this is not sufficiently nutritious and may harbour all sorts of weeds, pests or diseases.

CARE OF HOUSEPLANTS

For healthy growth a plant needs water and light, nutrition, good ventilation and a comfortable temperature. It derives energy for growth by photosynthesis – the action of light on chlorophyll, a green pigment in leaves and stems. Proper nutrition depends upon an intake of water and minerals from the soil, and carbon dioxide and oxygen from the air. These elements, in varying quantities, are essential to every plant.

Careful watering of houseplants should become a routine, but not one that is applied even-handedly and at the same time every week or month. You can tell if a plant needs water by checking the compost. The intake of moisture is affected by the size and growth-rate of the plant, the current stage of its annual cycle and the extent of the root system within the pot. More plants are lost through incorrect watering than any other cause and, unfairly, it makes no difference to the plant's decline if overwatering is actually a sign of the owner's good intentions.

Plants need more water when in active growth than during periods of rest. For many houseplants this means the most generous watering during spring and summer, but seasonal care is reversed for some winter-flowering plants. Flowering plants should be kept moist throughout the active season, whereas foliage plants can be allowed to dry out partially between waterings. Large plants usually need more water than smaller specimens, but fast-growing plants of any size are typically the most thirsty. A pot-bound plant has less compost to retain moisture and should be checked frequently for dryness. Succulent and fleshy-leaved plants are the least demanding as they store water they cannot immediately use.

Test the compost by scratching into it with your fingertip. Water a flowering plant in active growth when the top layer of compost has dried to no more than 2·5cm (1in) below the surface. Foliage plants come to no harm if the compost is allowed to dry up to one-third or one-half of its depth, and in winter this rule can also be applied to flowering plants that are resting. Some foliage plants prefer to be almost dry while they are inactive, and the compost of any plant should be made no more than barely moist in winter, as waterlogging occurs more quickly and is most damaging in cold conditions.

The majority of houseplants can be watered by the method of soaking the compost from the top. Pour in water at the base of the plant, using a small, long-spouted watering can to avoid splashing leaves or flower buds. Let the water drain right through the pot and after half an hour empty out the drip tray, so that the pot is not left standing in water.

Saintpaulia, Cyclamen and Gloxinia are among the plants that react badly to water on the leaves. You can water these by filling

In situations where it is difficult to maintain adequate humidity on a permanent basis, some plants will benefit from being misted with tepid water from a hand-held sprayer. Make sure the plant is one which will tolerate water on its leaves.

the drip tray and allowing the compost to take up water by capillary action. Empty out any water left in the drip tray once the compost is moist right through. Be cautious when watering decorative pots without drainage holes – those containing bulbs, for example. Pour off any excess as soon as the water stops sinking into the compost.

A parched plant in dry, crumbly compost can be revived, provided no root damage has occurred, by immersion. Peat compost must be immersed if it has dried right out because it shrinks and hardens, so water poured in from the top simply bypasses the rootball. Let the pot stand in water up to two-thirds of its height, until the compost surface glistens with moisture. As peat-based compost is light it may be necessary to hold or weight the pot until some water has been absorbed.

A trough of gravel is an attractive container for a group of pot plants, as well as providing a practical solution to the problem of keeping the atmosphere humid. The water level should alsways remain below the bases of the pots.

Ordinary tap water is perfectly suitable for most plants, but hard water may leave a lime deposit on top of the compost, forming a crust that prevents water from draining through. This can be scraped away and replaced by a top-dressing of fresh compost. Tap water may be very cold in the winter months, so fill the watering can before attending to the plants and let it stand for a while at room temperature.

Few plants enjoy a dry atmosphere and dry heat shrivels leaves and encourages insect pests. In such conditions, which may be caused by central heating or fine summer weather, you should take steps to improve the humidity of the plant's immediate environment. For a single specimen plant, this can be done by placing the pot in a larger container and packing the space between the two with moist peat. For a group of plants, the best method is to stand them on a layer of wet pebbles in a tray or trough. The bases of the pots must be above water level so that they do not actually take up moisture into the compost. Separately potted

Cleaning the leaves of a plant helps to prevent dust blocking the pores, so that it will stay healthy as well as looking fresh.

Use a soft paintbrush for delicate plants, or a soft, moist cloth for large-leaved specimens such as this Philodendron.

plants can also be packed into damp peat inside a trough. A direct way of giving more moisture is to mist leaves with tepid water from a plant spray. Water on leaves can cause spotting and withering in some species, so check first that this treatment is suitable for your plants.

The simplest way of feeding houseplants is to add a liquid feed to their water. Plants need food most during a period of active growth; resting plants take none at all. Check the manufacturer's directions about diluting the feed – usually only a few drops are needed in a can full of water. Never drop undiluted feed into dry compost – it can burn the plant's roots. Potting mixtures contain nutrients, and a freshly potted plant is adequately supplied for three to six months. Overfeeding is as damaging as overwatering. Brown, wilting leaves are a sign of this condition, while a plant with insufficient nourishment will develop small leaves and pale colouring. Some undernourished plants benefit from a foliar feed sprayed over the leaves, but this is first aid for a neglected plant, not a regular feeding routine. Sticks or pellets of plant food can be pushed into the compost and nutrients are dispersed when the plant is watered. With this method you cannot control the release of food according to the time of year. If the food stick is too close to the roots there is a danger of overfeeding or localized root damage; if it is at one side of the pot the essential minerals may not circulate evenly through the root-ball. Feeding mats are preferable as they supply nutrients to the base of the pot (the strongest roots usually occupy the lower third of the compost) and can be removed in winter to allow the plant to become inactive.

Note that tropical plants may not have a natural rest period, since conditions in their original habitat change little through the year. In a temperate climate these plants should be encouraged to rest and regenerate, so reduce watering and feeding as you do for other plants.

Keep plants and compost fresh by removing fallen leaves and dead flowers. Dust is damaging to foliage – it is not only unsightly, it also blocks the pores of leaves and masks light. Dust large or shiny leaves, supporting them in one hand while wiping them gently with a moist, soft cloth. Remove dust from frondy or velvety leaves using a soft paintbrush.

Proprietary leaf-shine liquids are available and they can be used in moderation on sturdy-leaved plants. Always follow the manufacturer's instructions to the letter, and if you are in any doubt about a particular plant's reaction to the chemical, try it out on a single inconspicuous leaf before you apply it to the whole plant. Never oil leaves to make them look glossy and never use detergents for cleaning.

Pinch out growing tips of bushy plants at the start of a new season of activity. Fast-growing plants can be pruned vigorously to keep a good shape and encourage strong growth, and should be cut back severely at the end of the active period. Cut straight across the stem, above a leaf node or newly budding leaves. Thin out tangled or crossed stems as these may restrict full growth and can trap fallen leaves, which then rot and can cause disease on otherwise healthy plants.

Green shoots may appear on variegated plants, and this indicates poor light. Cut any all-green shoots out as soon as they are noticed, otherwise the entire plant will revert to the same state. Obviously it will help if you then move the plant to a position where the light is better.

When you go on holiday the ideal solution to plant-care problems is to find a good friend who can cater to their needs. For plants left alone, there are several possible arrangements. If the holiday is short, water the plants thoroughly and pack the pots in moist peat. Put small plants, freshly watered, into polythene bags to trap the moisture. Use plant sticks to prevent the polythene from pressing on delicate leaves. You can buy a watering mat, to be placed on the kitchen draining board with one end in the sink. The mat draws up water from the sink and supplies it to the base of the pots. An alternative is to sink a long wick of soft string or thick wool into the compost in each pot and gather the wicks into a jug or bowl of water. Judge watering carefully if you leave plants alone over a winter holiday. It is probably enough just to water them thoroughly before you leave home. Move them away from cold areas near the windows, but make sure they are not deprived of adequate light.

A watering mat which draws up water from the kitchen sink will prevent your plants from drying out while you are away on holiday. Capillary matting suitable for this is obtainable commercially, and can keep plants going for quite long periods.

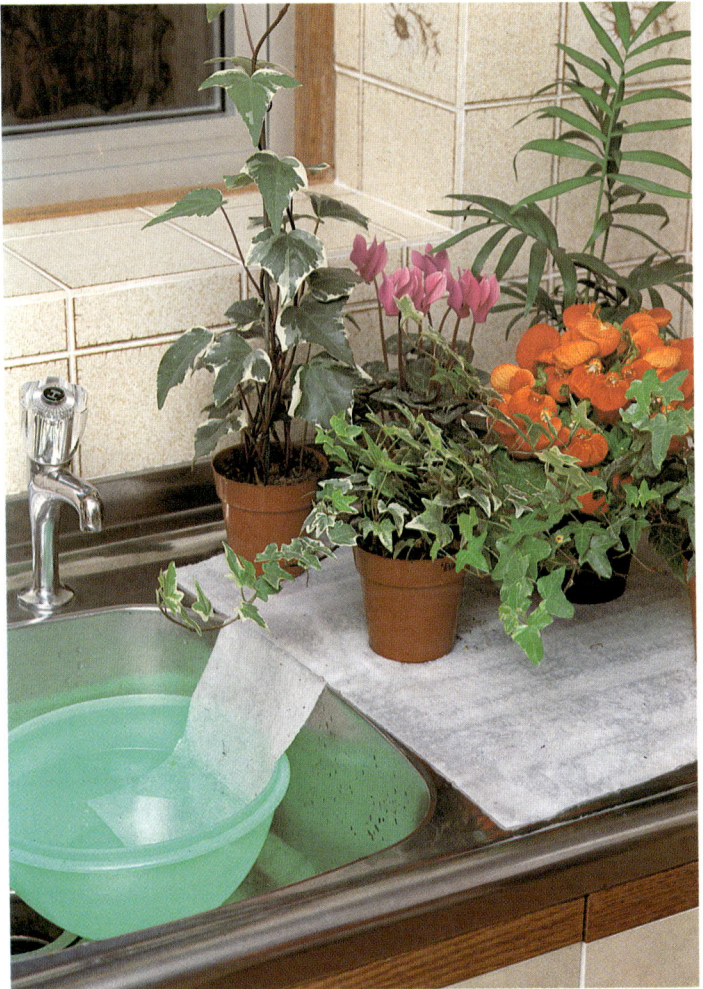

REPOTTING AND POTTING ON

A plant is repotted to provide fresh compost when the original potting mixture is becoming exhausted, or potted on to a larger container to give roots extra space for continuing growth. Potting on is not an automatic feature of plant care: several plants flourish most vigorously when slightly pot-bound, and the popular Sansevieria can stay in the same pot until the roots literally burst out of it. If a plant has become obviously top-heavy for its pot, or if the growth-rate has noticeably slowed or the foliage seems limp and lifeless, check that the compost is not dried out or waterlogged and that the plant is not exposed to cold air, before taking it out of its pot to examine the roots.

Roots escaping from a drainage hole are not a sure sign that a plant is pot-bound; there may still be plenty of space around the sides of the pot. To examine the root-ball, place one hand over the top of the potting mixture, with the plant's main stem or the base of a rosette plant held loosely between forefinger and middle finger. Turn the pot upside down and tap the base sharply. If the roots are firmly wedged, don't wrench them out. Tap the rim of the pot all round, squeeze the sides of a plastic pot or, as a last resort, carefully run a knife blade around the edge of the potting mixture. This gentle loosening of the root-ball is always necessary with large plants.

If the roots are densely matted and spiralled at the base of the compost, the plant should be potted on to a larger pot, but not too large or excess compost becomes over-moist and sour. If the

Firm the new compost lightly with the fingers, then water well and keep in a lightly shaded position for a few days.

Repotting a small plant, in this case a Coleus seedling: trickle compost gently round the sides of the plant.

Pot-bound roots: if a plant has filled its pot with roots it probably needs repotting, *although this is not always the case – some plants actually prefer to be pot-bound.*

roots are healthy and not crowded, gently shake off loose compost and replace the plant in its original pot with fresh potting mixture. Put a shallow layer in the bottom of the pot to support the plant at roughly the same height as before in relation to the pot rim. Trickle fresh compost down the sides, tap the pot to settle it and firm it down. Fill a small pot to within 1·2cm (½in) of the rim and a large one to 2·5cm (1in) below. Don't pack the compost tightly enough to prevent ventilation and good drainage. Water the plant thoroughly and make sure the water drains right through.

Repotting is best carried out at the beginning of a period of active growth. Annual and fast-growing plants may need potting on more than once in a year. Do not disturb a sick or resting plant; it cannot adjust to new conditions and even a healthy plant may seem sluggish for a few days after repotting. Don't anxiously try to water and feed it into activity during this period, as this will do more harm than good. It should recover within a week.

A plant in its maximum pot size, or one which seems a little slow but is not pot-bound, can be top-dressed to freshen the compost and provide extra nutrients. Scrape the top layer of compost with a spoon or small trowel and remove the loosened soil. Put in a layer of fresh potting mixture and firm it down. Only the largest palms and specimen plants will need a pot more than 25cm (10in) diameter, and these only after several years of growth.

PROPAGATION

There are several ways to raise new plants from old stock. The simplest method is to take stem cuttings from recent growth – this can be successfully achieved with a wide range of soft-stemmed plants. Stems from fast-growing plants, such as Impatiens, Pelargonium and Tradescantia, quickly develop into sturdy new specimens. Woody stems are slightly more difficult to set, and heel cuttings are used. Begonias, Saintpaulias and Gloxinias are among those that can be multiplied by whole leaf cuttings – a single leaf with the stalk attached.

For a stem (or tip) cutting, find a strong stem with a clean growing tip – choose non-flowering shoots, or pinch off buds and flowers. Cut the stem horizontally below a leaf node – the slight swelling on the stem from which leaves sprout – to a length that includes three leaf nodes between the cut end and the growing tip. Remove lower leaves so there will be none on the section of stem that is planted below the compost.

Fill a pot with one of the potting mixtures specially formulated for cuttings and make a small hole with a plant stick to receive the cut end of the stem. Press the compost gently around the stem and water it moderately.

A heel cutting from a woody plant consists of a side-shoot detached with a small spur of bark from the main stem. Pot up heel cuttings in the same way as stem cuttings, but first dip the heel end in hormone rooting powder. Plant a whole leaf cutting by inserting the leaf stalk into the potting mixture. Sansevieria can be propagated from rectangular leaf sections cut across the width of the leaf and sunk to half their depth in compost. Note that new plants will lose the variegation of the parent, reverting to green.

Keep cuttings in moderate conditions until new growth indicates that rooting is successful. To protect them, you can cover the pot with a plastic bag, which will hold warmth and moisture, or keep them in a propagator. Resist the temptation to pull up the cutting to see if roots have started. If you are really in doubt that it is growing, pull very gently on the stem – if there is any resistance the roots have begun to anchor the plant. A failed cutting will eventually wither, but leaves may drop anyway, so give it good time to get started. When cuttings have rooted, pot up the new plants separately, allow them a few days to adjust before exposing them to full light or a change of temperature, and then treat them as you did the parent plant.

Some plants produce small offsets or plantlets at the base, on stems or on leaf edges. These can be detached and settled in potting mixture to root. A few plants will seem to divide naturally when you take out the root-ball for repotting. If this happens, you can pot up the sections separately.

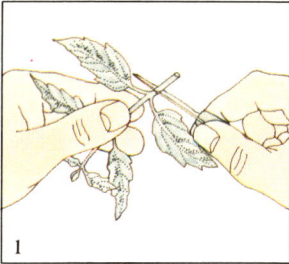

Stem cuttings: 1 trim stem to just below a leaf joint; 2 dip in hormone rooting powder; 3 insert in compost with the aid of a dibber, and 4 protect the whole pot in a plastic bag. Leaf cuttings: 5 and 6 insert 5cm (2in) sections top end uppermost in the potting mixture. For whole leaf cuttings, 7 insert stalks into holes made with a dibber, and 8 firm the compost around them.

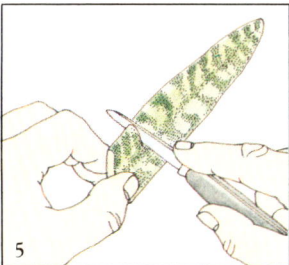

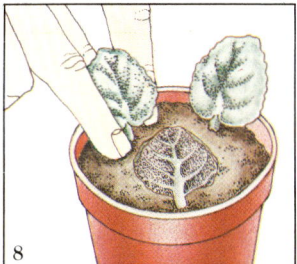

WHAT CAN GO WRONG

Some plants are more vulnerable to insect attack than others and certain conditions, such as dry heat, encourage insect pests. However, problems with houseplants are usually due to the wrong kind of care, not necessarily neglect, and root-rot or fungus diseases typically take hold in plants that are overwatered or too cold. Such ailments can quickly become irreversible, so if a plant begins to look sickly or fails to grow during its most active season, check that it has the right environment, and that the compost is neither parched nor waterlogged, before worrying about pests and diseases.

It is more difficult to correct overwatering than to compensate for underwatering, although some delicate houseplants cannot be revived after drying out completely. Waterlogged roots must be allowed to breathe; an added problem here is that plants dislike being disturbed unnecessarily, so to take an already ailing plant out of its pot may compound the damage. But if the plant has really suffered through overwatering, you may want to take the risk, as it will otherwise die anyway. Remove it gently from its pot (see p. 28) and examine the roots. If they are discoloured and the outer layers of tissue pull away easily, the plant may be too far gone to recover. Remove any rotted, brown roots and put the plant in a clean pot with fresh, dry potting mixture. Don't water it again until you see signs of resumed growth and from then on take care to water moderately and keep an eye on the plant's condition.

Overfeeding the plant can cause wilting and discoloured leaves. When you suspect this problem, the plant will come to no further harm if you reduce feeding for a while to see if it recovers. Take special note of the fact that newly repotted plants probably have sufficient nutrients in the compost for a whole season's growth.

Not only the roots, but also the crown or stems of the plant may have begun to rot if it is too wet. Often such cases must be thrown away, but if the trouble has not gone too far, cut out the diseased areas and repot the plant. Cool, moist conditions may encourage botrytis, a grey fluffy mould which can appear anywhere on the plant, including on flowers and buds. A less common fungal disease is mildew; leaves are spotted or fully coated with a white, powdery deposit. In either case, cut away the diseased sections of the plant and treat it with a fungicide, as directed by the manufacturers.

Sooty mould is also a fungus; as the name suggests, it shows up as a black deposit on the leaves. This is not due to poor care or bad conditions, it is a sign of insect attack. Wipe away the mould with a clean damp cloth and inspect the plant for aphids, whitefly or mealy bug.

Aphids, commonly known as greenfly, and whitefly are sap-sucking insects. They leave a honeydew deposit on leaves and

It is not difficult, given a little experience, to diagnose the commonest of the problems that can beset houseplants. In most cases inadequate or incorrect routine care is being administered, and this can often lead to attack by diseases or infestation by insect pests. The following guidelines may help you to identify the cause of any problems, but for more specific advice on the care of individual houseplants, check their cultural requirements in the A-Z section of this book. Underwatering can result in wilting leaves that become shrivelled and brown. Overwatering leads to drooping leaves, rotting stems and waterlogged roots. Underfeeding leads to slow and spindly growth, while overfeeding may show up in wilting and discoloured leaves. Common diseases are sooty mould which appears as black blotches on leaves, and botrytis which appears as grey fluffy mould. The commonest pests are aphids which manifest themselves in the form of a sticky honeydew secretion, mealy bugs which deposit a white cottony fluff, and red spider mite which produces a white webbing under the leaves. Plants kept in conditions which generally do not suit them will begin to look unhealthy sooner or later, and pest and disease attack will hasten their deterioration.

stems and the sooty mould develops on this. The insects weaken the plant, which may show stunted growth or yellowing leaves. Check buds, growing tips and the undersides of leaves, and if you find the tiny green or white insects, spray the plant with an insect-icide, following the manufacturer's directions. Red spider mites are similar pests that thrive in warm, dry conditions. If you cannot see the insects themselves, you may notice a fine white webbing on the undersides of leaves.

Mealy bugs may attack the leaves and stems or roots of a plant. They are white, lice-like creatures that cling to the plant tissue. Root mealy bugs can be treated by insecticide watered into the compost. Those found on leaves and stems can be wiped off, and periodic spraying will be necessary to control the problem.

Remember to wear rubber gloves when treating a plant with chemicals. Insecticides and fungicides can be sprayed on or water-ed into the potting mixture, depending upon their composition, so check the instructions. Several applications over a period of weeks may be advisable to be sure of eradicating the problem. Insect pests are less common than fungus diseases in houseplants, but it is important to treat an affected plant right away, or other plants will become infested.

Plants that have happily adapted to conditions in your home may yet be subject to problems you have not anticipated. Aerosol sprays, such as furniture polish or hair lacquer, can be troublesome to plants. If mysterious spotting appears on leaves and does not spread, it is possible that you have unintentionally sprayed the plant with something it finds unpleasant. Pets can cause problems, knocking over pots or bruising the plants in passing – cats, for example, may chew the leaves of houseplants. Plants put outside during summer may be troubled by worms that have got into the pots. They do little real damage but worm casts in the soil can block drainage holes and cause waterlogging.

WHAT CAN GO WRONG

Wilting or total collapse of whole plant	Excessive heat Overwatering or underwatering Infestation or rotting of roots
Falling leaves	Low temperatures or draughts Overwatering
Falling flower buds or failure to flower	Poor light
Brown discoloration of leaf tips	Bruising Overwatering or overfeeding Lack of humidity
Pale leaves or loss of variegation	Poor light
Spindly growth	Excessive heat Poor light Too much moisture
Dry, discoloured patches on leaves	Underwatering Sun scorch
Soft, discoloured patches on leaves	Overwatering Water splashed on leaves
Yellowing, spotted or withering leaves	Overwatering Low temperatures Insect attack
Rotting of stems or crowns	Overwatering Fungus disease
Sticky or spotted leaves	Insect attack
Soft black patches on leaves	Sooty mould caused by insect attack
Grey, furry mould on leaves	Botrytis
White powder on leaves	Mildew
Stunted or distorted growth	Insect attack in roots or stems

ACALYPHA HISPIDA

CHENILLE PLANT

This fast-growing shrub, which at full height reaches at least 75cm (2½ft), has large, oval, bright green leaves, and in summer and autumn it develops showy red flower spikes that droop gracefully among the foliage.

To get the best display, give the plant bright light, but shield it from direct sun. Keep the compost moist, watering more in summer than in winter, and apply a liquid feed every two weeks in the growing season. A warm position, minimum 15°C (60°F) is important, but dry heat causes leaf-fall, so create a moist environment and mist leaves regularly from early spring until flowering is about to begin. Repot in spring, using rich, loam-based compost. Acalypha develops a broad spread, so cut back stems after flowering. It may be preferable to discard a plant that has grown too large, rooting new plants from stem or heel cuttings, taken in spring and potted in a peat and sand mixture.

Special note
Pinching out growing tips is unnecessary and may delay flowering

| Easy to grow |
| Light position |
| Warmth and moisture |
| Summer and autumn |

ACHIMENES

CUPID'S BOWER

Achimenes grows from a cluster of small rhizomes, each of which sends up a single stem bearing heart-shaped, toothed, dark green leaves. Flaring tubular flowers are profuse from summer to autumn, though individual blooms last only a few days. The many hybrids offer flowers of white, pink, red, yellow or purple. Fine stems tend to trail as they grow longer, and may be up to 60cm (2ft) long.

In spring and summer give the plant bright light, with three to four hours of morning or evening sun each day during flowering. A warm temperature, minimum 13°C (55°F), and high humidity are necessary. Water moderately with tepid water and feed fortnightly. After flowering, reduce watering and cut back stems to compost level, leaving the plant dry over winter. Freshen the compost and resume watering in early spring. New rhizomes are produced each year; separate them and pot up clumps of four or five together.

Special note
Dislikes lime; if possible use soft water or rainwater

Needs extra care
Bright position
Warmth and humidity
Summer and autumn

ADIANTUM

MAIDENHAIR FERN

This is one of the most popular ferns, though not the easiest to grow. It is an attractive plant with fine black stems and fresh, delicate-looking foliage. There are several species and cultivars, growing from 30 to 60cm (1 to 2ft) tall. The fronds are erect when young, but droop gracefully as they grow longer.

Maidenhair ferns like a warm environment and tend to go dormant if the temperature is below 13°C (55°F). They do equally well in a light or partially shaded position, protected from direct sun. Provide a moist atmosphere, especially in warmer temperatures, but be wary of spraying the leaves, which can react badly. Keep the root-ball moist at all times and give a fortnightly liquid feed in spring and summer. Reduce watering in winter. Pot in loam or peat-based compost and pot on only when roots appear above the surface. Start new plants in spring by dividing the rhizome base.

Special note
Dryness shrivels the fronds but too much moisture rots the roots

Needs extra care
Light or partial shade
Warmth and humidity
All year round

AECHMEA

URN PLANT

The leaves of Aechmea form a rosette with a natural cup at the centre, from which a flower spike emerges in spring. *A. fasciata* has grey-green, coarse leaves with broken bands of white. These grow up to 60cm (2ft) long and arch gracefully outwards. The flower spike has pink bracts which last up to six months, and develops small blue flowers, but these quickly fade. A rosette flowers only once, then gradually dies back and is replaced by new offsets growing around the base.

Give Aechmea strong light and a warm temperature – over 16°C (50°F). Create a humid atmosphere and spray the leaves frequently. Moisten the compost and keep some water in the central cup, freshened every three weeks. Peat compost is best, and the plant rarely needs repotting. Offsets can be detached or allowed to take over from the parent rosette, which can be cut back as it dies.

Special note
Prefers soft water; if possible use freshly collected rainwater to moisten the cup

| Easy to grow |
| Bright position |
| Warmth and humidity |
| Spring and summer |

AGLAONEMA

PAINTED DROP TONGUE

The foliage is the main attraction of Aglaonema, though white or yellow flower spathes appear in summer and autumn. Spear-shaped leaves, patterned in silver or cream, rise from a central stem which may develop into a fleshy trunk in older plants. The leaves are up to 38cm (15in) long, but the plant is quite compact.

The main requirement for this plant is a warm temperature, with an absolute minimum of 13°C (55°F) at night and in winter. In high temperatures keep up a good level of humidity. Aglaonema tolerates partial shade – shield it from direct sun. Keep the compost moist throughout the year, watering less in winter to give the plant a rest period. Feed monthly while in active growth. Pot on young plants in spring, but they are best kept with confined roots in a maximum pot size of 15cm (6in). A mature plant can be divided while it is being repotted.

Special note
Keep aglaonema away from the fumes of heating appliances

| Easy to grow |
| Light or partial shade |
| Warm conditions |
| All year round |

ANTHURIUM

FLAMINGO FLOWER

A. *andreanum* and A. *scherzerianum* are the flowering species; both have leathery, pointed, deep green leaves which grow up to 20cm (8in) long on narrow stalks. The common name describes the flowers which have a twisted spadix, like a long neck, surrounded by an apron-like coloured spathe: this is usually red or orange, but cream, pink or yellow cultivars are sometimes seen.

Anthurium must be warm at all times, minimum temperature 16°C (60°F). Bright, filtered light or a position in a window away from direct sun is best for flowering. High humidity also encourages flowers; these usually appear in summer but in good conditions can come at any time of year. Never let the root-ball dry out, and use tepid water to moisten compost and spray leaves. Pot in a coarse, open mixture of peat with sphagnum moss or leafmould. The root system is small; pot on up to a 15cm (6in) pot, and divide a large plant.

Special note
Must be kept moist, but beware of overwatering. Dry air causes leaf curl

| Needs extra care |
| Light position |
| Warm conditions |
| Flowers in summer |

ASPIDISTRA

CAST-IRON PLANT

This tough, tolerant plant has a sheaf of dark green, leathery leaves rising from a rhizomatous base. There is a cultivar with leaves attractively banded with cream. The plant is slow-growing, up to a height of 50cm (20in) with a 30cm (12in) spread.

An Aspidistra will quietly survive in poor light and cool or warm temperatures, but to get the best show of foliage, provide average light with no hot sun, a minimum temperature of 10°C (50°F) and a fairly humid atmosphere. Water moderately in spring and summer, allowing two-thirds of the compost to dry out between waterings, and feed occasionally. Keep the root-ball just moist in winter. Sponge away dust from the leaves but do not use leaf-shine chemicals. Pot in soil-based compost – it rarely needs repotting – and create new plants by dividing the rhizome, taking sections with at least two leaves attached.

Special note
Brown marks on the leaves are a sign of overwatering

| Easy to grow |
| Light or partial shade |
| Cool or warm position |
| All year round |

AZALEA INDICA

INDIAN AZALEA

These decorative shrubs bloom in spring under natural conditions but cultivated varieties appear in flower from autumn through the winter. The leaves are oval and dark-green; flowers may be single- or double-petalled, in white or shades of pink and red. Some cultivars have streaked petals. The plants achieve a height and spread of about 45cm (18in).

Azaleas like bright light but do not need or like direct sun. Cool temperatures and high humidity encourage flowering. Mist the leaves frequently and keep roots moist all year round. The plant greatly dislikes lime, so use soft water or fresh rainwater. Pinch off dead flowers and repot the plant in peaty compost after flowering ceases. Put it outdoors in summer, in a shady position, and keep it moist and fed. Bring it indoors before nights become frosty and give it a cool environment to start it into flower.

Special note
Hot, dry air causes
buds to fall without
opening

| Needs extra care |
| Light position |
| Cool moist conditions |
| Winter and spring |

BEGONIA

There are literally hundreds of Begonia species and varieties, including attractive foliage and flowering plants. *B. semperflorens*, the Wax Begonia, is a popular flowering type, having clusters of small pink, white or red flowers and glossy bright green or bronze leaves. *B. glaucophylla* is a cane-type Begonia, developing sprawled stems that are shown off well in hanging baskets. *B. hiemalis* is a bushy plant, glossy-leaved with rich red flowers. *B. rex* is the best known foliage Begonia; it has large, heart-shaped leaves in deep green patterned with pale green and red.

Give Begonias bright light, indirect or with morning or evening sun. Keep a minimum temperature of 13°C (55°F) and a fairly moist atmosphere. Water moderately through spring and summer, sparingly in winter, and give a fortnightly feed while the plants are in active growth. Stem cuttings from most types root easily.

Special note
Flowering Begonias
tend to become leggy
or sprawling; cut back
the stems to preserve
a good shape

| Easy to grow |
| Light position |
| Moderate conditions |
| Winter or summer |

BELOPERONE GUTTATA

SHRIMP PLANT

The plant's common name refers to its drooping bracts, graduating from red-brown at the base to pale green at the tips, which encase fine, white flowers. Beloperone grows to a height of about 45cm (18in) with several slender stems bearing fresh green leaves. Bracts and flowers appear for up to ten months in the year.

To encourage flowering, give plenty of light and a warm position during active growth from spring to autumn; keep the compost moist and feed the plant fortnightly. Water sparingly in winter and provide an even, cool temperature. Use loam-based compost to pot on young plants each spring, to a container one size larger. Top-dress more mature plants. Control the plant's tendency to leggy, sparse-leaved growth by pinching out growing tips and pruning stems quite radically in early spring. The pruned stems can be used as cuttings to start new plants.

Special note
Remove a few bracts from a young plant to encourage bushy growth

| Easy to grow |
| Light position |
| Moderate conditions |
| Spring to autumn |

CALADIUM

ANGEL'S WINGS

This plant also has the common name of Elephant's Ears, which effectively describes the shape of its large, colourful leaves. There are many hybrids, and colours include white leaves with green veins, green marbled with red, or red and pink edged with green. Each leaf is carried on a separate stalk and may be up to 30cm (12in) long, and thin and papery but quite resilient.

Provide a bright position out of direct sun – leaf-colours fade in poor light. Maintain warm temperatures and high humidity; spray the leaves frequently and pack pots in moist peat. Water well in spring and summer, giving occasional weak feeds. Pot the plant in peat compost and make sure it is free-draining. When foliage dies down in winter, store the tuber almost dry and in complete shade. To start new growth in spring, keep it warm and resume watering.

Special note
Draughts or sudden
cold will make the
leaves crumpled and
weak

| Needs extra care |
| Light position |
| Warmth and moisture |
| Foliage spring-autumn |

CALCEOLARIA

SLIPPER FLOWER

These are bright plants, bought for a single season's display. The curiously pouched flowers last for a month or so; they are pink, red, orange or yellow, attractively spotted with dark red. A rosette of large green leaves surrounds the flower stems. Most cultivars grow to a total height of about 30cm (12in).

Give the plants bright light, filtered or sunless; a north-facing window is a good spot. Keep them cool and in a humid atmosphere, since both conditions prolong flowering, but do not spray the foliage. Water them generously and, if necessary, pot on into a larger container, using loam-based compost. Look out for aphids, which can trouble the flower buds and growing tips.

Special note
Keep thoroughly moist;
if the soil should dry
out, immerse the pot
in water as soon as
possible

| Easy to grow |
| Light position |
| Cool conditions |
| Flowers in spring |

45

CAMPANULA

ITALIAN BELLFLOWER

Campanulas are known and loved as garden flowers, but the indoor variety, *C. isophylla*, is a delightful plant for pots or hanging baskets. It has a dense, trailing growth habit – small, bright leaves with toothed edges and star-shaped, pale blue flowers which appear in midsummer and autumn. *C.i.* 'Mayi' is a cultivar with more intense blue-mauve blooms, and the flowers of *C.i.* 'Alba' are white. Trailing stems grow up to 50cm (20in) in length.

The plant needs bright light and a cool, well-ventilated position. Keep the roots very moist in spring and summer, and feed fortnightly. Cut back the stems close to compost level after flowering and water sparingly through winter. Repot in spring, or when roots appear on the compost surface, but only to a maximum pot size of 12·5cm (5in) diameter. Take short tip cuttings in spring.

Special note
Pinch off fading blooms to encourage a prolonged flowering period

| Easy to grow |
| Light position |
| Cool conditions |
| Summer and autumn |

CEROPEGIA

HEARTS ON A STRING

C. woodii is the only Ceropegia grown as a houseplant. Thread-like, trailing stems, growing up to 1·8m (6ft) long from a tuberous base, bear heart-shaped, fleshy leaves, paired at intervals of about 7·5cm (3in). The leaves are green marbled with white on the upper surface, purple on the underside. The fine stems can be trained to climb on a miniature trellis set in the pot.

Ceropegia requires good light at all times and some sun to maintain leaf coloration. It thrives in normal room temperature and tolerates a dry atmosphere, as the succulent leaves store water. Keep the compost barely moist, watering only enough to prevent it from drying out completely. Pot on small plants in spring, providing a mixture of soil and sand to ensure good drainage. Older plants can stay in a pot only 10cm (4in) in diameter for several years.

Special note
Poor light causes sparse leaf growth, with longer intervals of bare stem

| Easy to grow |
| Light position |
| Moderate conditions |
| All year round |

CHAMAEDOREA ELEGANS

PARLOUR PALM

This attractive plant has the classic palm shape – arching stems bearing pairs of narrow, tapering leaves. It is slow-growing while young, eventually reaching a height of 1·3m (4ft) with individual stems up to 1m (3ft) long.

It dislikes direct sun but grows spindly and tired in poor light, so provide a position with filtered light or partial shade. Chamae-dorea tolerates a wide temperature range, but prefers warmth during active growth and a cooler environment in winter. Keep the atmosphere moist, misting leaves occasionally, but do not use leaf chemicals. Water moderately in spring and summer, with a half-strength feed once a month. In winter the compost should be kept barely moist. Use a free-draining compost, peat or loam, or a mixture of the two. Repot only when roots fill the pot, up to a size of 20cm (8in) and thereafter top-dress the established plant.

Special note
Make sure the compost never dries out completely. Warm, dry air may encourage red spider mite

| Easy to grow |
| Light or partial shade |
| Moderate conditions |
| All year round |

CHLOROPHYTUM

SPIDER PLANT

The most popular indoor variety is *C. comosum variegatum*, well-known for its arching, grassy leaves, striped in green and cream. During its active season the Spider Plant produces long flower stalks; the small white flowers are quickly replaced by plantlets that will hang in profusion from a healthy, mature parent plant. It may grow up to 1m (3ft) high and wide and is best displayed in a hanging basket or on a pedestal.

Chlorophytum tolerates shade, but the leaf colours are most pronounced if it is grown in bright light. It also accepts a wide range of temperatures, from 7°C (45°F) minimum up to 27°C (80°F). Water generously from spring to late summer and feed fortnightly. It grows very fast, in peat or loam compost, and may need repotting more than once in a year. The hanging plantlets look attractive, but can be detached and potted up separately.

Special note
Brown leaf tips may be
due to lack of moisture.
Cut them out if they
become too noticeable

| Easy to grow |
| Light or partial shade |
| Cool or warm position |
| All year round |

CHRYSANTHEMUM

Chrysanthemums sold as pot plants are cultivars or hybrids of *C. morifolium*. They are specially treated to dwarf the growth and produce plants in flower at any time of year, though they are naturally short-day plants. The average height is about 30cm (12in). The broad, ragged-edged leaves may be bright or dark green; flowers in white, yellow, pink or a range of warm colours from flame through red to purple can last six weeks or more.

The essential points of care for these temporary plants are to keep the compost thoroughly moist and maintain a cool temperature. Warm conditions shorten the flowering period; protect the plant from direct sun, and increase humidity if it is kept above 16°C (60°F). Remove dead flowers and when flowering ceases, plant out the Chrysanthemum in the garden where, if it takes, it will resume its natural tall growth habit.

Special note
Buds will fail to open
in poor light or
over-warm conditions

| Easy to grow |
| Light position |
| Cool conditions |
| Short flowering season |

CISSUS

KANGAROO VINE

C. antarctica is a popular and widely available houseplant that can grow up to 3m (10ft) high, forming a dense screen of rich green foliage. Individual leaves are pointed ovals with lightly toothed edges. The plant may gain as much as 60cm (2ft) in one year's growth. It has tendrils that enable it to climb, and should be given strong support from an early stage.

Grow Cissus in a light or partially shaded position; direct sun can cause transparent blotches on the leaves. It likes moderate warmth in summer and a cooler rest period in winter. Spray the leaves if the atmosphere is dry. Keep the compost moist during the active season, watering when the top layer of soil has dried out. Give a liquid feed every two weeks, or a weaker solution with every watering. In winter just moisten the potting mixture. Pot on each spring, in loam-based compost, up to a 25cm (10in) pot.

Special note
Pinch out growing tips
to encourage a bushy
spread and cut back
one-third of the growth
each spring

| Easy to grow |
| Light or partial shade |
| Moderate conditions |
| All year round |

CITRUS MITIS

CALAMONDIN ORANGE

This attractive plant is appreciated as an unusual addition to a houseplant collection. *Citrus mitis* can grow up to 1·3m (4ft) high, though it is not likely to exceed 1m (3ft) indoors. It is shrubby with glossy, dark green, oval leaves. White fragrant flowers appear in summer, followed by small oranges, though a well cared-for plant may produce fruit or flowers at any time.

Give the plant the brightest possible position, in normal room temperatures. It will tolerate a winter minimum of 7°C (45°F), though little growth will occur below 13°C (55°F). Water moderately in spring and summer, sparingly in winter. Regular feeding is essential from spring to autumn. All aspects of growth are improved if the plant is placed outdoors in summer. Pot on in spring as necessary, in loam-based compost. Pinch out growing tips and remove long shoots to keep a compact shape.

Special note
The plant is vulnerable to insect attack in dry conditions, so keep up a good level of humidity

| Easy to grow |
| Bright position |
| Moderate conditions |
| All year round |

CLIVIA

KAFFIR LILY

This striking plant has a fountain of strap-like, dark green leaves radiating in layers from a central growing point. In late winter the flower stalk rises through the rosette, and in spring as many as fifteen trumpet-shaped, orange blooms develop. The flower stalk is up to 45cm (18in) high and the foliage spread may be 1m (3ft).

Provide Clivia with bright light to encourage flowering, but not hot sun. Allow average warmth during the active period but a cool rest period in winter, when compost should be kept almost dry. Resume watering as flower stems develop, then keep the compost moist from spring to autumn and add a fortnightly liquid feed. The plant flourishes best if slightly pot-bound, top dressed with a soil-based compost. Offsets grow among the roots; these can be detached and potted up, or left to develop into masses of fine foliage and multiple flower heads.

Special note
Cut off each flower head as it fades and remove a whole stem when it withers

| Needs extra care |
| Bright position |
| Moderate conditions |
| Flowers in spring |

COCOS NUCIFERA

COCONUT PALM

This plant can reach a height of 1·3m (4ft) indoors but it is extremely slow-growing. The narrow leaflets give the fronds a ribbed appearance; they are shiny and dark green and the stems spread out from a central base.

The Coconut Palm will tolerate partial shade but may do better in a light position. Never subject it to direct sun, and be careful not to let it dry, or the fronds will shrivel very quickly. Water the compost moderately at all times, less when the temperature is low. A temperature range from cool to warm is acceptable, but provide a winter minimum of 10°C (50°F). Mist the leaves when the surrounding air is warm. Established plants can be given a weak liquid feed at every watering. The plant hardly ever needs repotting; top-dress with soil-based compost and pot on only if the base begins to rise out of the pot.

Special note
Brown spots on the foliage indicate overwatering or sudden exposure to cold

| Easy to grow |
| Light or partial shade |
| Moist conditions |
| All year round |

CODIAEUM

CROTON

There are many varieties of Codiaeum, presenting a marvellous choice of decorative foliage. Leaves may be straight or broad, lance-shaped or oval, undulating, indented or deeply cut. All are variegated in a range of patterns including marbling, veining, spots and blotches and in colours from green to yellow, red, pink and bronze. They are generally bushy plants, growing up to 1m (3ft) high with a 60cm (2ft) spread.

Leaf colours develop most vividly in bright light, but the plant should be shielded from hot direct sun. A warm temperature, minimum 16°C (60°F), is essential and the higher the temperature, the more humidity is needed. Water generously and feed fortnightly from spring to autumn. If the roots dry out, lower leaves will fall. Pot on each spring, in loam-based compost, up to a 25cm (10in) pot. Take cuttings from side-shoots and keep them very warm and moist.

Special note
If the plant gets too large, cut back stems in early spring. New growth will quickly appear

| Needs extra care |
| Bright position |
| Warm conditions |
| All year round |

COLEUS

FLAME NETTLE

These brightly coloured foliage plants are favourites for warm window sills and group displays. The soft leaves are heart-shaped or slender ovals, richly variegated in combinations of green, yellow, red, pink, orange and bronze. The plants grow up to 45cm (18in) tall, but are best kept pinched out for a bushy habit up to 30cm (12in) high.

Provide the brightest possible position – in a south- or west-facing window – but shield leaves from hot midday sun. A warm, moist atmosphere is best; the leaves wilt and quickly die if they are cold. Water generously in spring and summer and give fortnightly feeds. It can be difficult to overwinter these plants; if kept for a second season, cut back growth and repot in early spring. Even in a single season plants may need frequent repotting as roots spread very quickly. Stem cuttings take easily.

Special note
Coleus dislikes hard water; if possible, use freshly collected rainwater to mist leaves and moisten compost

Easy to grow
Bright position
Warm conditions
Best in spring/summer

COLUMNEA

GOLDFISH PLANT

The most popular Columneas are C. × *banksii*, a hybrid with stems up to 1·3m (4ft), smooth green leaves and scarlet flowers, and C. *microphylla*, with hairy leaves and scarlet flowers inset with yellow, on stems growing as long as 2·4m (8ft). Both are densely-leaved trailing plants showing masses of flowers in spring.

Give them a position with good light but no direct sun, average warmth but a cooler winter temperature. Columnea requires high humidity, especially in centrally heated homes. Mist the leaves frequently and keep the compost moist throughout the year, though barely moist in winter. Dilute liquid feeds to half-strength. The plant is shallow-rooting and does well in loam or peat, mixed with sphagnum moss. Pot on only when roots fill the container. Cut back untidy growth in autumn. Take cuttings after flowering, rooting three or four together in a mixture of peat and sand.

Special note
Use only tepid water to spray leaves; cold water causes staining

Needs extra care
Light position
Warm conditions
Flowers in spring

CORDYLINE

CABBAGE PALM

Cordyline has a strong central stem and a loose rosette of arching leaves. C. *terminalis* has spatulate red and green leaves fanning out from the stem on stalks. The cultivar 'Red Edge' has green leaves streaked with red-purple radiating directly from the stem.

Provide a humid atmosphere at normal room temperatures, or up to 21°C (70°F) during the day, and a bright position not under direct sun. Keep the compost thoroughly damp during the season of active growth; moisten it sparingly in winter. The plant will benefit from a fortnightly feed in spring and summer. Pot on each spring in a soil-based compost, until the plant is in a 25cm (10in) pot. Then top-dress the potting mixture at the start of each new growing season. Lower leaves that dry and wither can be pulled off. A tip cutting kept warm and protected under plastic will root in about four to six weeks.

Special note
Dry air can turn the leaves brown and papery; maintain a humid atmosphere

| Needs extra care |
| Light position |
| Warmth and humidity |
| All year round |

CRASSULA

JADE PLANT

This genus of succulents includes several different plants, all vigorous and long-lasting. C. *argentea* is the Jade Tree, with a sturdy, upright 'trunk' and spoon-shaped shiny green leaves. C. *arborescens*, Chinese Jade, has branching stems bearing fleshy green leaves tinted with red. In C. *falcata*, called the Propeller Plant, extended grey-green leaves grow in a twisting arrangement usually concentrated on one main stem. It also develops clusters of scarlet flowers in late summer.

Good light and a temperature range from cool to warm suit these plants. They should be watered moderately and fed every two weeks in active growth, kept barely moist in winter. Pot on every other year, providing a mixture of three parts soil to one part sand, to ensure good drainage. Stem cuttings taken in spring should be kept warm and moist and fed monthly until rooted.

Special note
Poor light causes pale,
drawn out growth

| Easy to grow |
| Light position |
| Moderate to warm |
| All year round |

CYCLAMEN

POOR MAN'S ORCHID

Cyclamen is a winter-flowering plant, in season from September to December, but with many hybrids available it may be possible to find a plant in flower at any time of year. Each leaf and bloom is carried on a separate stalk; the height and spread of the plant is about 30cm (12in). The leaves are heart-shaped and dark green, usually marked with silvery bands. Flowers may be single or double blooms, with finely curved or frilled edges, and in a colour range through white to pink, red or purple.

Provide a cool position with bright light. Water moderately from below, or around the tuber where it shows above the compost. Never mist the leaves, as this will mark them. Plants are often discarded after flowering, but can be taken on by allowing growth to die back and keeping the tuber dry until autumn, when it can be repotted in loamy soil.

Special note
When removing fading
flowers take out the
whole stalk, not just
the bloom

| Needs extra care |
| Light position |
| Cool conditions |
| Flowers 2-3 months |

CYPERUS

UMBRELLA SEDGE

C. alternifolius has tall, rushy stems topped by an umbrella of radiating green leaves and thin, grassy flower heads. It grows between 45cm (18in) and 1m (3ft) tall. There is a cultivar with white-streaked leaves, and a dwarf variety, *C. diffusus*.

Cyperus originates from swamp conditions and likes to be thoroughly wet at the roots. Stand the pot in a saucer or shallow dish and keep it topped up with water. This also takes care of humidity in the surrounding air. Normal room temperatures are acceptable, minimum 10°C (50°F) in winter or at night. It grows happily in full light or partial shade, but fewer stems grow if the light is poor. Pot on in loam-based compost when the clump of stems fills the pot. Divide a large plant and keep to a 12·5cm (5in) maximum pot size, as the roots are best confined and the plant's slender base seems unbalanced in a wide container.

Special note
Browning leaf tips indicate dryness or crowded roots that need repotting

Easy to grow
Light or partial shade
Wet conditions
All year round

DIANTHUS

MINI CARNATION

Dianthus have for years been among the most popular garden plants for borders and small flower beds, but they are relative newcomers as pot plants. They have a delicate appearance, with feathery foliage and small pretty flowers in white, pink or red, sometimes marked near the centres with darker-toned rings. They are grown for a single flowering season indoors but can be planted out in the garden when the growth has died back in autumn.

Keep these plants in a bright, airy place, in moderate conditions, preferably on the cool side. They appreciate some sunshine, but do not leave a plant behind window glass under hot midday sun. Water the compost evenly throughout the flowering season and give a weak feed fortnightly. There should be no need to repot the plant, but if it seems cramped, pot on in loam-based compost.

Special note
Make sure the compost
drains freely; the plant
should be kept moist
but not wet

Easy to grow
Bright position
Moderate conditions
Flowers in summer

DIEFFENBACHIA

DUMB CANE

Among the different varieties of Dieffenbachia the fleshy leaves, broadly lance-shaped and growing from strong, cane-like stems, may be marked with cream, white or yellow. The markings are sometimes so pronounced that only the leaf-edges are green. The plant can grow to 1·3m (6ft) if not confined; lower leaves fall as it ages. It is called Dumb Cane because its poisonous sap can cause painful swelling and temporary loss of speech if brought in contact with the mouth; wear gloves when pruning or repotting the plant.

Provide a bright position with mild winter sun or filtered summer rays. Warmth and humidity are essential conditions. The plant has no definite rest period; water moderately at all times and feed only if new growth is being produced. Pot on each spring in loam-based compost. Limit growth with a maximum 20cm (8in) pot or continue potting on up to a 30cm (12in) container.

Special note
Supplement short
daylight hours in winter
with fluorescent light
at night

Easy to grow
Light position
Warmth and moisture
All year round

DIZYGOTHECA

FALSE ARALIA

This plant has a woody central stem and toothed, leathery leaflets fanning out on separate leaf stalks. Leaves are coppery when young but later turn a very dark green. A slow-growing plant, it eventually develops a tree-like habit and may grow up to 1·8m (6ft) tall with a 1m (3ft) spread. It is usually sold as two or three young plants potted together, to give a bushy appearance.

The plant's environment must be warm and humid, with good light, but no direct sun. Water the compost sparingly at all times; avoid overwatering but keep the root-ball moist. Supply weak liquid feeds fortnightly through spring and summer. Repotting, in soil-based or peat compost, is only necessary every two years, up to a 25cm (10in) pot. From then on top-dress the compost every spring. Propagation is best left to specialists, and young plants are readily available.

Special note
Leaves drop if the plant is kept too wet or too dry, leaving an unsightly length of bare stem

Easy to grow
Light position
Warmth and moisture
All year round

DRACAENA MARGINATA

DRAGON TREE

D. marginata is single-stemmed with a fountain of narrow green leaves, striped at the edges with red-purple. It can reach a height of at least 1·3m (4ft) indoors; as it ages the lower leaves fall, leaving an attractively scarred, woody 'trunk'. The variegated form D. m. 'Tricolor' has pink and cream stripes. Other Dracaenas vary in shape and colour and may have less height and a broader spread; they are less tolerant than D. marginata.

Provide a warm position with bright light, protected from hot, direct sun. Dracaena tolerates cool conditions for short periods and will grow in partial shade, though the leaf colours may fade. Create a humid atmosphere, and spray foliage occasionally with tepid water. Keep the compost thoroughly moist except in winter, and feed every two weeks while there are signs of active growth. Pot on each spring, or as roots fill the pot, in a soil compost.

Special note
Dracaena enjoys the warmth of a centrally heated home, but be sure to provide high humidity

| Easy to grow |
| Light position |
| Warmth and moisture |
| All year round |

ERICA HYEMALIS

CAPE HEATHER

Erica provides a welcome touch of colour in winter months, but it is not easy to keep long-term as a pot plant, so plants are often discarded after flowering. It has shrubby growth, up to 60cm (2ft) high; erect woody stems carry tiny fine leaves, densely massed. The small tubular flowers are rose-pink at the base, shading to white tips. Hybrids offer different colour choices.

It is important to keep the plant cool: a maximum temperature of 13°C (55°F) is essential. Place it in a brightly lit position with no hot sun. Keep the compost thoroughly moist and provide a high level of humidity, misting the leaves frequently. Use lime-free distilled water or rainwater whenever possible. To take the plant on for a second year, cut it right back after flowering and leave it outdoors during the warmer months, keeping it shaded and very moist.

Special note
Central heating is fatal to this plant; in hot dry air it will fade and shrivel in no time

| Needs extra care |
| Light position |
| Cool conditions |
| Flowers in winter |

FATSIA JAPONICA

CASTOR OIL PLANT

This broad-leaved plant needs a spacious position; it is quick-growing and reaches 1·3m (4ft) with a 1m (3ft) spread in only two years. It has palmate leaves, spreading but deeply cut into seven or nine fat 'fingers'. The most common form has bright green, glossy foliage, but there is a cultivar with cream variegation.

Provide good light, protected from direct sun: growth is spindly and pale if the light is too poor, but the plant adapts to partial shade. Cool temperatures produce the most resilient foliage, though a warm environment is acceptable if it is quite humid. Spray leaves with tepid water but do not use leaf-shine chemicals. Keep compost moist throughout the year and feed an active plant fortnightly. Repot in soil-based compost every spring, up to a 25cm (10in) pot. Growth is more vigorous once a large pot size is reached, but do not overpot a young plant.

Special note
Pinch out growing tips if young plants are not branching, and prune growth severely in spring

| Easy to grow |
| Light position |
| Cool conditions |
| All year round |

FICUS ELASTICA

RUBBER PLANT

The Rubber Plants commonly available now are the cultivars 'Robusta' and 'Decora', both having large, shiny, bright green leaves on a sturdy central stem. Another cultivar, 'Tricolor', has attractive cream and pink blotches on the leaves. All are tough and tolerant plants, growing up to 3m (10ft) tall.

Bright light and moderate warmth are the best conditions, but Ficus will adapt to low light and cooler temperatures, minimum 13°C (55°F). Water moderately from spring to autumn, letting the compost dry to half its depth between waterings. Give a liquid feed every two weeks. Sponge the leaves occasionally to clear dust. In winter, water only enough to keep the root-ball moist. Pot on young plants in spring, in a soil-based compost, but keep the plant's roots slightly confined. When it has reached a 30cm (12in) pot, top-dress the potting mixture in following years.

Special note
The lower leaves of older plants fall as the stem thickens; in young plants leaf fall indicates overwatering or too much heat

| Easy to grow |
| Light position |
| Warm conditions |
| All year round |

FITTONIA

SNAKESKIN PLANT

Fittonia is a low-growing plant, up to 15cm (6in) in height, but it has a creeping habit and may spread to 30cm (12in) or more across. Oval green leaves are attractively netted with silver or red veins, depending upon variety. *F. argyroneura* 'Nana' is the smallest plant of this genus, but the least demanding.

The most important growing conditions are an evenly warm temperature – preferably around 18°C (65°F), minimum 13°C (55°F) – and a very humid atmosphere. Double-pot with a layer of moist peat and spray the leaves frequently. Fittonia prefers subdued light and will tolerate quite a shady position. Water the compost regularly but with caution; the plant is very sensitive to being too wet or too dry. Pot in a small container, using peat-based compost. It is shallow-rooting and does not need frequent potting on. Take stem cuttings in spring, four or five to a pot.

Special note
The growth of creeping plants tends to straggle; cut back stems severely in spring

| Needs extra care |
| Partial shade |
| Warmth and moisture |
| All year round |

FUCHSIA

LADY'S EARDROPS

There is a large number of Fuchsia varieties, from tall standards with a strong central stem to erect bushy plants and elegant trailers. All have pointed or oval, bright green leaves and fine, drooping, bell-shaped blooms in rich tones of red, pink or purple. The plants may be up to 1m (3ft) tall with a broad spread. They live happily outdoors in summer, in tubs or hanging baskets.

Fuchsias should have the best available light, with some sun to encourage flowering. They prefer a cool to moderate temperature range and an airy position. Keep the compost moist and leaves misted while the plant is in active growth. When leaves drop in winter keep the plant in a cool room until new growth starts. Repot in loam-based compost, prune back one-quarter of the growth and subsequently pinch out the growing tips to maintain a bushy shape. During flowering, remove fading blooms.

Special note
Flower buds dropping are a sign of too much moisture

Needs extra care

Light position

Moderate conditions

Flowers in summer

GREVILLEA

SILK OAK

This is a fast-growing evergreen that can reach a height of 1·8m (6ft) in under two years. It has a drooping, slightly feathery appearance. The foliage, which is brown-tinged when young, gradually coarsens with age. Grevillea is often used as a tall focal point for a grouped arrangement of plants.

In poor light the plant will shed its leaves, so it needs a light position, but one protected from direct sun in summer. In winter move it closer to a window. A tolerant plant, Grevillea prefers a cool environment but tolerates warmth providing it has adequate humidity. Water the compost thoroughly but allow the top layer to dry out between waterings. Feed weekly if growth is particularly vigorous. In winter the soil can dry out to half its depth, but the plant's root-ball must always be moist. Repot annually up to the maximum convenient size and then top-dress the soil.

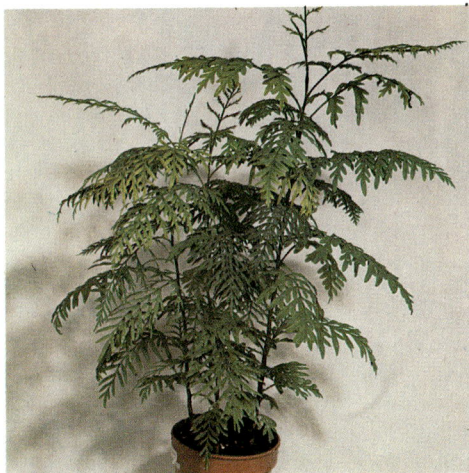

Special note
When pruning, cut back the branches but do not remove the leading growth of the main stem

| Easy to grow |
| Light position |
| Cool conditions |
| All year round |

GUZMANIA

ORANGE STAR

In common with other bromeliads, Guzmania has a rosette of leaves forming a natural cup at the centre; unlike other popular types, the leaves are soft and ribbon-like rather than tough and fleshy. They are a glossy, rich green marked with fine red lines. In winter a flower spike grows from the cup; it consists of red or orange bracts that last a few months; short-lived flowers, white or yellow, arise from the bracts. The plant grows about 38cm (15in) tall; the leaves arch gracefully outwards.

Bright light, a warm environment and continuous moisture are the requirements of this plant. Keep compost moist and also pour water into the cup and over the foliage from time to time, adding a liquid feed every two weeks except during flowering. The plant is shallow-rooting and may not need potting on. Offsets growing at the base can be detached and potted up in spring.

Special note
Browning, shrivelled leaves are a sign that the air is too dry around the plant

| Needs extra care |
| Bright position |
| Warmth and moisture |
| Flowers in winter |

GYNURA

VELVET PLANT

There are two Gynuras commonly sold as houseplants – one has erect stems and large, toothed oval leaves; the other is a smaller trailing plant. The leaves of both bear rich purplish hairs that show up well in sunlight, and they are fast-growing if given good conditions. Small orange flowers appear in summer; they smell extremely unpleasant and should be picked off while still in bud.

Bright light and some direct sun are necessary to preserve the purple colouring of the leaves. A minimum temperature of 13°C (55°F) and high humidity are the best conditions. Water moderately, to keep the compost continually moist, but give less water if the temperature is cool. Gynuras become untidy after two years or so; pinch out tips to encourage bushiness, but discard a straggling plant, using the stems for tip cuttings which will root in gritty compost if kept warm and barely moist.

Special note
Provide a moist atmosphere but do not spray the leaves, as this may cause spotting

Easy to grow
Bright light
Moderate conditions
All year round

HEDERA

IVY

There are many varieties of small-leaved Ivies bred from *H. helix*, the Common Ivy. They are vigorous plants that trail or climb, and may be variegated with cream, white or yellow. *H. canariensis*, Canary Island Ivy, is a popular species with larger leaves that are heavily marked with cream and grow on red stems. Varieties of *H. helix* cling naturally, but *H. canariensis* must be tied to or interwoven with its support.

Variegated Ivies need some bright light, filtered or indirect as the sun's hottest rays can cause scorching. They tolerate a broad range of temperatures and should be given a more humid atmosphere in an environment over 18°C (65°F). Water moderately at all times and reduce watering in winter months to allow a brief rest. Pot on if roots emerge through the drainage holes of the pot. Prune the growth as necessary and use the pruned stems as cuttings. These root in water or moist, loam-based compost.

Special note
Hot dry conditions are encouraging to insect pests which may attack ivy plants

| Easy to grow |
| Light position |
| Cool or warm |
| All year round |

HELXINE

MIND YOUR OWN BUSINESS

This plant is a pretty diversion from other types of houseplants. It is tiny-leaved and low-growing, but with a broad and rapid spread, and practically takes care of itself. Foliage is bright green or golden and very delicate in appearance.

Give Helxine a position in bright light or partial shade, but no direct sun. It thrives in cool or moderate conditions, but cannot tolerate warmth above 21°C (70°F). Keep the compost permanently moist, but never wet. Add a weak liquid feed once a month and mist the foliage occasionally during spring and summer. The plant is shallow-rooting and will hardly ever need repotting. Trim stem ends as necessary to control the shape – snipped stems root readily in peat, or the plant can be divided and sections placed on top of moist compost, where they quickly root into the soil.

Special note
Be careful to water underneath the foliage, which is easily crushed by a rapid flow of water

| Easy to grow |
| Light or partial shade |
| Cool or moderate |
| All year round |

HIBISCUS

CHINESE ROSE

This branching shrub can grow up to 1·8m (6ft) but for indoor cultivation it can be kept pruned back, and modern hybrids will flower when only 38cm (15in) tall. The dark green, glossy leaves of Hibiscus may be oval or undulating at the edges; flowers, which appear from spring through to autumn, are trumpet-shaped but open out broadly to 12·5cm (5in) across. They can be found in white, pink, yellow, orange or red, single- or double-petalled.

In warm months Hibiscus is happy in normal room temperatures, but likes a cool winter rest at 13°C (55°F). Provide a bright position with some sunlight. Water generously during active growth, supplying a weak feed at every watering, and mist foliage with tepid water. Pot on lively specimens as necessary, in loam-based compost. In late winter prune back half the previous year's growth. Take heel cuttings from side-shoots in spring.

Special note
Poor light, dry air
or sudden draughts will
cause the flower buds
to drop

| Easy to grow |
| Bright position |
| Warm conditions |
| Spring to autumn |

HIPPEASTRUM

AMARYLLIS

Hippeastrums are usually sold as dry bulbs during the dormant winter period, but are sometimes available potted up, with flower buds developing. These appear in late winter or early spring. The hollow stem eventually shoots up to about 75cm (2½ft) and bears two to four large flower trumpets, in white, red or orange. Leaves follow the flower buds, appearing naturally in early spring, but bulbs are sometimes forced for Christmas flowering.

While the flowers are developing Hippeastrum needs good light and some direct sun, average warmth and constant moisture. Feed fortnightly at this time. Reduce watering as flowers fade and stop altogether when foliage dies down in mid-autumn. Keep the bulb dry for ten to twelve weeks, then freshen the potting mixture, disturbing the roots as little as possible, and resume watering.

Special note
Leave foliage in place
until autumn

Easy to grow
Bright position
Warm conditions
Spring/early summer

HOYA CARNOSA

WAX PLANT

Both the leaves and flowers of this elegant climbing plant have a waxy texture. Leaves are dark green ovals; star-shaped white or pink-tinged flowers appear in summer, in thick clusters each growing from a woody spur. Hoya will not flower until it is two or three years old. It is vigorous and can grow very tall. Train stems on a hoop or trellis, but do not prune the plant.

For the active growth period from spring to autumn, Hoya needs bright light with a few hours each day of mild morning or afternoon sun. Average room temperatures are suitable and high humidity is preferred; mist-spray leaves with tepid water, except while the plant is in bloom. Water thoroughly but let the compost dry partially between waterings. In winter, rest the plant in a cool position and barely moisten the compost. Keep it slightly pot-bound; pot on only when necessary, in a loam-based compost.

Special note
Do not remove the
woody spur that carries
a flower cluster; it is the
source of the following
season's blooms

Easy to grow
Bright position
Warm conditions
Flowers in summer

HYDRANGEA MACROPHYLLA

HOUSE HYDRANGEA

Indoor Hydrangea varieties have woody, branching stems, broad oval leaves up to 15cm (6in) long and large, fat flower heads consisting of clustered small florets. They bloom in spring; flowers are pink or purple in alkaline soil, turning blue if soil is acid. It can be difficult to obtain successful flowering in a second year, so these plants are usually treated as temporary, but can be planted out in the garden after a season indoors.

Place a Hydrangea in a cool position, bright but sunless. Mist the foliage occasionally and keep the compost permanently moist. If it dries out, immerse the pot in water, but even if the plant revives the flowering period will be shortened. Dry heat also limits flowering. A plant placed outdoors all summer, brought in and kept cool, shaded and almost dry in winter, may flower again indoors. Growth should be pruned back severely after flowering.

Special note
High humidity
encourages flowering,
discourages insect pests

| Easy to grow |
| Light position |
| Cool conditions |
| Spring and summer |

HYPOESTES

POLKA DOT PLANT

The species sold as a houseplant is *H. sanguinolenta*, meaning 'blood-spotted', and Hypoestes is very popular for its decorative foliage, olive-green dappled with pink. Small lilac flowers may appear in summer, but these are usually insignificant. An older plant will become straggly and the maximum effective height is about 35cm (14in), when stems may need some support. Pinching out of growing tips encourages bushy growth, but Hypoestes is generally regarded as a short-lived plant and discarded when leaf-growth becomes sparse.

The plant grows quickly and should be potted on as necessary in loam-based soil. Water moderately at all times and mist the leaves to maintain humidity. A warm temperature is required, as is good light to preserve the leaf markings. Take stem cuttings, keeping them warm and moist, to replace an ageing plant.

Special note
Dry compost will
cause leaf fall; keep
the soil evenly moist,
but not wet

| Easy to grow |
| Light position |
| Warmth and moisture |
| All year round |

IMPATIENS

BUSY LIZZIE

There are many hybrid strains of these cheerful, fast-growing plants. According to type, the succulent stems may bear bright green or bronze leaves and the flat, five-petalled flowers appear in a range from white through pale pink to red, coral, orange and mauve. The recently developed 'New Guinea' hybrids have multi-coloured foliage. They are now often regarded as annuals, but can be grown on for a second year.

Bright light is vital for flowering, which is continuous through spring and summer. Water generously when the plants are in active growth and feed regularly. Moderate watering is the rule for plants resting in winter. Do not leave them standing in water or allow compost to dry out completely. Pot on as necessary, but Impatiens flower most freely when slightly pot-bound. Prune stems at any time to encourage a bushy shape. Stem cuttings root easily.

Special note
Protect the plant from
harsh, drying sun and
from low temperatures

| Easy to grow |
| Light position |
| Warm conditions |
| Spring and summer |

JASMINUM

JASMINE

Jasmine has a delicate appearance, with slender, climbing stems bearing small green leaves and tubular white or pink flowers, but it is not a difficult plant to grow. Flowering occurs from December to April. Overall growth can be up to a height of 1·8m (6ft) but can be pruned and trained to a suitable size and shape.

Water the plant generously while it is in active growth and give a fortnightly feed. Reduce watering as flowering ends and then let the plant rest, with barely moist compost and no food. Thin out and prune stems that have flowered. A bright, relatively cool environment is best at all times – about 16°C (60°F) with a winter minimum of 7°C (45°F). Repot in spring, as necessary, in a loam-based compost. Jasmine enjoys a period outdoors in summer months; mist the foliage of plants kept indoors. Tip cuttings taken in spring or autumn will root in a peat and sand mixture.

Special note
Train the long fine stems around a wire hoop set in the compost

| Easy to grow |
| Light position |
| Cool conditions |
| Winter/early spring |

KALANCHOE

FLAMING KATY

The flowering Kalanchoë is *K. blossfeldiana*, a rosette plant up to 35cm (14in) in height, with fleshy, dark green leaves and clusters of small red flowers borne on tall stems. Flowering is from late winter to early summer, though plants may be forced into early flowering for sale at Christmas time.

A bright position with some sun encourages a good show of flowers. Keep Kalanchoë in a moderate environment – a south-facing window in winter, east- or west-facing in spring and summer are ideal locations. Water it sparingly at all times and feed every two weeks while in flower. After flowering, trim back the growth and let the plant rest in partial shade, with the compost barely moist, for about one month. It is a short-day plant and will not bloom a second season if kept too light in between times. Repot in a soil mixture, in a larger pot only if this seems necessary.

Special note
Do not mist-spray the plant or drop water on the leaves

| Easy to grow |
| Light position |
| Moderate conditions |
| Winter/early summer |

KENTIA FORSTERIANA

KENTIA PALM

There is only one other species in this genus, *K. belmoreana*, the Sentry Palm. The two plants are similar for indoor cultivation; they are slow-growing and should not exceed 1·8m (6ft). Arching, dark green fronds rise on leaf stalks from a central stem; the leaflets are long and broad and push up almost vertically from the stalks to create a lush spray of foliage.

Kentia Palms tolerate low light, but prefer filtered light or only partial shade. The minimum winter temperature should be 10°C (50°F) but in summer the palms accept temperatures as high as 27°C (80°F) and are tolerant of dry air, though a moist atmosphere improves leaf texture. Sponge leaves gently to clear dust but do not use a chemical cleaner. Kentias do not have a noticeable rest period; water compost moderately all year round. Pot on every two or three years, in soil-based compost, up to a 25cm (10in) pot.

Special note
As lower leaves turn brown with age, cut them off. Patchy leaf browning indicates cold or overwatering

| Easy to grow |
| Light or partial shade |
| Warm conditions |
| All year round |

LILIUM LONGIFLORUM

EASTER LILY

The Easter Lily has a tall stem, up to 1m (3ft) high, topped by trumpet-shaped white or speckled blooms with a heavy fragrance. Leaves are strap-like, spreading horizontally at intervals up the stem. It may be bought as a dry bulb, or in spring as a full-grown plant about to flower.

Pot a dry bulb in autumn, in a 15cm (6in) pot and a rich soil potting mixture. Leave the tip of the bulb showing above the surface. Keep it cool, moist and shaded until growth develops. Then move it to full light and a slightly warmer position, but protected from direct sun. Keep the compost moist around a growing plant and feed it regularly when flower buds begin to show. After flowering let growth die back and rest the bulb, repotting in the autumn. Growth is less luxuriant in a second year, so alternatively it can be planted out in the garden after one season indoors.

Special note
The plant can be given extra encouragement to flower if daylight is supplemented by fluorescent light in the evenings

| Needs extra care |
| Light position |
| Cool conditions |
| Flowers in spring |

MARANTA

PRAYER PLANT

There are several different cultivars of Maranta sold as houseplants. The popular name of Prayer Plant refers to their common habit of folding up their leaves at night. Other names, such as Herringbone Plant or Rabbit's Tracks, indicate the type of leaf markings to be seen. The broad oval leaves, up to 12·5cm (5in) long, grow on stalks from a sheathed stem and spread outwards rather than upwards.

Marantas must have warm, moist conditions; maintain a minimum temperature of 18°C (65°F) if possible, though 10°C (50°F) is just tolerated in winter. Low light is preferred – sunshine fades the leaves. Water generously from spring to autumn, sparingly in winter and supply weak liquid feeds during active growth. Spray or sponge leaves, but do not apply leaf chemicals. Pot on each spring, if necessary, in loam-based compost – the plants are shallow-rooting. Divide large clumps during repotting.

Special note
Dry air causes leaf drop; give constant humidity

Needs extra care
Low light/part shade
Warmth and moisture
All year round

MONSTERA DELICIOSA

SWISS CHEESE PLANT

Always among the ten most popular houseplants, the Swiss Cheese Plant is so called for its huge glossy leaves, deeply cut or perforated from edge to centre. It lasts many years and will grow to a height of 3m (10ft), but can even double that size in time. It also has a very broad spread, with mature leaves up to 60cm (2ft) across, and will need the support of canes or a sturdy pole.

From spring to autumn give the plant indirect light or partial shade and moist conditions. Water and feed it well, keeping the compost moist but not wet. In winter it needs less water and can tolerate full light. Keep leaves dust-free by sponging them gently. Repot the plant every two years in loam compost coarsened with grit or leaf-mould. Top-dress a plant already in a large pot. Aerial roots develop from the plant's main stem; tie them to the stem and train them down into the compost.

Special note
Young leaves are uncut, but if they fail to develop incisions the light is too poor or the plant undernourished

Easy to grow
Light or partial shade
Moist conditions
All year round

NEPHROLEPIS

BOSTON FERN

N. cordifolia grows fronds up to 60cm (2ft) long; *N. exaltata* has a wider spread, each frond up to 1·3m (4ft). The fronds are broad at the base, tapering to pointed tips, and and have paired, smooth-edged leaflets. There are cultivars with frilled or cut leaves.

A light position with no direct sun is best, but Nephrolepis tolerates poor light for a few weeks at a time, especially if it is supplemented by fluorescent light. Provide high humidity in normal room temperatures and mist leaves frequently. Keep the compost moist all year round, but reduce watering in cool conditions. Below 10°C (50°F) the plant will cease growing and may die. Pot on when roots fill the pot, in a coarse peat or loam mixture. Feed a plant potted in peat more generously than one in loam. Runners spreading from the plant's rhizome base put down small plantlets, which can be detached and potted up separately.

Special note
Cultivars may revert to growing smooth-edged fronds; cut them right out or they will dominate the growth

Easy to grow
Light position
Warmth and moisture
All year round

PASSIFLORA

PASSION FLOWER

There are many species in this genus, but only one is sold as a houseplant – *P. caerulea*, an exotic-looking plant which is easy to grow, being wiry and quite vigorous. It is a climber that needs the support of a hoop or canes. It has starfish-shaped leaves and elaborate flowers, consisting of yellow centres surrounded by long filaments shading through purple, white and blue, which are backed by white petals. These are sometimes followed by fruits in autumn, but this is not common in plants grown indoors.

Passiflora needs bright light all year round and mild sun to promote flowering. Through the active growth period provide warm but well-ventilated conditions, water the compost generously and add a fortnightly feed. Rest the plant through the winter with the compost almost dry, then pot on in spring, if necessary, in a loam-based compost. Spring is also the time to carry out pruning.

Special note
If the plant fails to
set flower buds, keep it
slightly potbound and
stop feeding

| Easy to grow |
| Bright position |
| Warm conditions |
| Flowers in summer |

PELARGONIUM

GERANIUM

These fast-growing, bushy plants make a marvellous summer display with their bright flower heads, and many have attractively marked leaves. The rounded, bright green leaves of Zonal Pelargoniums are marked with a dark red band; flowers may be single or double, in light sprays or heavy clusters, white, pink, coral, red or mauve. The Regal Pelargonium flowers earlier and has a shorter season; it has showy, frilled flowers and clustered leaves. Smaller Ivy-leaved Geraniums are excellent for tubs or hanging baskets.

Bright light and plenty of sunshine are essential,. Provide a moderate environment, dry and airy; do not spray leaves or flowers. Keep compost moist in the active period and feed fortnightly. The plants thrive most vigorously if slightly pot-bound. Stem cuttings root readily in summer and can replace older plants. Prune growth severely in autumn, and allow the plant a cool winter rest.

Special note
Beware of overfeeding;
it will encourage a rich
mass of leaves instead
of flowers

| Easy to grow |
| Bright position |
| Moderate conditions |
| Flowers in summer |

PELLAEA ROTUNDIFOLIA

BUTTON FERN

This is a true fern, though not conforming to an expected fern-like appearance. The fronds of Pellaea grow up to 30cm (12in) long and form shallow arcs; the 'button' leaves are dark green, tough, and almost circular in shape. They grow densely, in pairs alternating up the narrow black stems.

Indirect light or partial shade suit this plant. It should never be subjected to direct sun. Normal room temperatures are quite suitable; between 10°C (50°F) and 16°C (60°F) it will show little growth. If the air is warm, spray foliage frequently to preserve adequate humidity. Pellaea is shallow-rooting; it can be grown in peat-based or loamy compost and needs potting on only when roots completely fill the pot. In peat compost it will need a fortnightly feed from spring to autumn; in richer loam, only monthly feeds. Keep the compost continually moist, but not wet.

Special note
Dry air or drying compost will cause the fronds to shrivel

Easy to grow
Light or partial shade
Warmth and moisture
All year round

PEPEROMIA

DESERT PRIVET

P. *magnoliifolia* is a compact plant about 30cm (12in) high, with oval, glossy, dark green leaves; there is a variegated form with yellow leaf-markings. P. *obtusifolia* is similar in its erect, bushy habit, but has purple stems and purplish leaf-margins. P. *caperata* is a more spreading plant with heart-shaped, heavily textured leaves and tall white flower spikes in summer.

Peperomias thrive in bright light with some mild sunshine. From a winter minimum of 13°C (55°F) they tolerate the range of normal room temperatures, but need high humidity if kept warm. Use tepid water to moisten the compost, which should be allowed to dry out partially between waterings. From spring to autumn add a half-strength liquid feed every two weeks. Pot in a peaty, soil-less compost but keep the plants confined. They rarely need re-potting and will live happily in a maximum 12·5cm (5in) pot.

Special note
Low humidity causes
loss of leaves, but this
reaction can also be
due to overwatering

| Easy to grow |
| Bright position |
| Keep cool or warm |
| All year round |

PHILODENDRON

SWEETHEART PLANT

Philodendrons are erect or climbing plants with tough, glossy leaves. The most popular is *P. scandens*, with heart-shaped, dark green leaves, each about 10cm (4in) long. *P. hastatum* has more elongated, almost triangular leaves. Both grow up to 1·8m (6ft) and need the support of canes or a sturdy pole. *P. bipinnatifidum* has erect stems and spreading, deeply cut leaves; it will grow to about the same total height as the climbers.

Philodendron will live in a bright but not sunny position, or in a lightly shaded spot. The absolute minimum temperature should be 13°C (55°F), but above this it tolerates a wide range. High humidity encourages strong growth. Water the compost moderately, allowing a winter rest period of near-dryness. Provide a weak feed with each watering while the plant is actively growing. Pot on when roots fill the containers, in a mixture of peat and loam.

Special note
Pinch out the growing
tips of *P. scandens* to
encourage bushiness;
straggly growth means
light is too dim

| Easy to grow |
| Light or partial shade |
| Warmth and moisture |
| All year round |

PILEA

ALUMINIUM PLANT

There are various forms of Pilea, which may be creeping or upright plants. The popular Aluminium Plant is *P. cadieri*; it grows to about 25cm (10in) in height and each leaf is marked with silvery patches between the veins, giving a quilted effect. *P. mollis* is more heavily textured and has rich bronze colouring around the leaf veins. *P. involucrata*, also known as the Friendship Plant because it is easily propagated, has warm, coppery colouring.

Pileas must never be exposed to direct sun and will adapt to indirect light or partial shade. They prefer to be kept warm and humid, tolerating a 10°C (50°F) minimum, but they are badly affected by draughts. Keep the compost moist, with a fortnightly feed from spring to autumn, and less damp in winter. Repot only if necessary – the plants are shallow-rooting – up to a 12·5cm (5in) pot. Stem cuttings in spring will root in a peat and sand mixture.

Special note
Will become straggly after 2-3 years; keep growing tips pinched out but replace an ageing plant

| Easy to grow |
| Light or partial shade |
| Warmth and moisture |
| All year round |

PLATYCERIUM

STAGHORN FERN

This unusual plant has branching fronds, mid-green with a rough-textured coating of white, sheathed at the base by an undivided, fan-shaped frond. In the wild it grows high up, clinging to tree bark. Although it may be sold potted in peat, the more natural way to grow it is attached to a piece of bark. Wrap the roots in damp sphagnum moss and wire or tie them to the bark, where they will soon take hold and become self-supporting.

Give the plant a spacious, well-ventilated position in indirect light or partial shade. It must be kept warm and moist; spray the fronds frequently. To water a bark-grown specimen, sink the bark in a bucket of water for about fifteen minutes, or less if the temperature is cool. A pot-grown plant will probably also have to be immersed, as the fronds wrap around the top of the pot. Add a liquid feed no more than once a month.

Special note
Keep the plant moist
but never wet; do not
detach it from its
support unless
absolutely necessary

| Needs extra care |
| Light or partial shade |
| Warmth and moisture |
| All year round |

PRIMULA

This genus includes several species of spring-flowering plants. They have fresh green, lightly toothed or scalloped leaves, forming a clustered base from which grow flower stalks bearing single blooms or multiple flower heads, depending upon the type. Some are annual plants, others for only temporary display indoors; *P. vulgaris* can be transferred to the garden after flowering. Maximum height for any Primula is 45cm (18in).

The colourful flowers need bright light at all times, with some mild sun. Provide a cool, moist, well-ventilated environment; flowers fade much more quickly in heated rooms. Keep the potting mixture thoroughly damp and feed once a week while the plant is in flower. Pot on small plants right away, into a 10cm (4in) or 12·5cm (5in) container, to give room for extra growth. Pick off flowers as they fade, taking out the whole flower stalk.

Special note
Keep several plants
together in a tray of
moist pebbles for a
flourishing, vivid
display

| Easy to grow |
| Light position |
| Cool conditions |
| Late winter/spring |

PTERIS

TABLE FERN

There are many plants in this genus but the most popular small ferns are *P. cretica* and its cultivars. *P. cretica* has bright green fronds consisting of slightly serrated, paired leaflets with one terminal leaf at the tip of the stalk. The variegated type 'Albolineata' is striped with cream; 'Rivertonia' has crinkled, feathery fronds. Each of these plants grows about 30cm (12in) tall and the fronds arch slightly.

These plants tolerate shade but are more vigorous in bright indirect or filtered light. They accept normal room temperatures, preferring a winter minimum of 13°C (55°F). Provide a humid atmosphere and spray foliage frequently. Keep the potting mixture thoroughly moist, but reduce watering in cool conditions. Pot in a peaty mixture and feed the plant fortnightly during the active period. Pot on in spring, but only if roots fill the pot.

Special note
If the leaves begin to shrivel or turn brown, there is not sufficient humidity in the air

Easy to grow
Light or partial shade
Warmth and moisture
All year round

RHOICISSUS

GRAPE IVY

This sturdy plant will climb vigorously if given the support of a trellis or a tripod of canes. A young plant can look good shown off in a hanging basket. The leaves of Rhoicissus are large and undulating at the edges. The cultivar 'Ellen Danica' has deeply cut leaves with serrated edges.

Rhoicissus is a tolerant plant; strong sun or sudden cold will be damaging, otherwise it thrives in indirect light or partial shade, cool or warm conditions. In a heated room, raise the humidity and spray leaves regularly. While the plant is in active growth keep the compost thoroughly moist and give a weekly feed. Reduce watering to a minimum in winter. Pot on each spring up to a 25cm (10in) pot; in later years top-dress the soil. Stem cuttings will root in a peaty mixture if kept warm and protected under plastic.

Special note
Pinch out growing tips in spring; if necessary, prune drastically to reduce the size

| Easy to grow |
| Light or partial shade |
| Keep cool or warm |
| All year round |

ROSA

MINIATURE ROSE

Indoor Roses are varieties or hybrids of the dwarf Rose *R. chinensis*. They make attractive, upright bushes, about 30cm (12in) high. The slender stems rarely carry thorns. Flowers may be single- or double-petalled, in white, pink, yellow, red or coral.

Miniature Roses must have as much light as possible. Place them in a bright window and, if possible, stand them close to a fluorescent light in the evening. They do well in a temperature range from 10°C (50°F) to 21°C (70°F) and like a fresh, airy atmosphere. They overwinter in cold conditions and can be placed outside. Move them from warm, bright summer light to cool winter shade by stages, for the best future growth. Water moderately during active growth and feed fortnightly. Keep the compost, a soil-based mixture, barely moist in winter. Prune back the stems and freshen the compost annually, just before new growth begins.

Special note
Cut back the stems as you remove dead flower heads; this acts as a continual pruning that encourages new buds

| Easy to grow |
| Bright position |
| Moderate conditions |
| Spring and summer |

SAINTPAULIA

AFRICAN VIOLET

The familiar rosette plants, with a mound of oval or round, slightly hairy leaves and cluster of bright flowers, are all hybrids of *S. ionantha*. In ideal conditions the plants will flower for up to ten months in the year.

Maintain a steady, moderate temperature, about 18°C (65°F) and provide as much bright light as possible, but protect leaves from direct sun. Water moderately for most of the year, giving weak feeds with every watering. Provide high humidity, but avoid wetting the leaves at any time. Allow a four to six week winter rest period – minimum temperature 13°C (55°F) and compost left almost dry. Saintpaulia is shallow-rooting and should be kept slightly pot-bound, in peat compost in a small container. Propagate by rooting whole leaf cuttings. When removing dead flowers or damaged leaves, take out the whole stalk down to the base of the plant.

Special note
To prolong flowering place near a fluorescent light source in the evenings

| Needs extra care |
| Bright position |
| Warm conditions |
| Spring to autumn |

SANSEVIERIA

MOTHER-IN-LAW'S TONGUE

Sansevieria's tall rosette of sword-shaped, fleshy leaves is very distinctive. It is a tolerant, slow-growing plant that will reach a height of about 1m (3ft). There are several cultivars, mainly bred from *S. trifasciata*, which has silver-grey bands on dark green leaves. Perhaps better known is *S. t.* 'Laurentii', whose mottled green bands are bordered with a bright stripe of yellow.

Sansevieria is extremely adaptable, but will suffer if too cold, and may cease growing in winter. Room temperatures of 16°C (60°F) to 27°C (80°F) are acceptable. Only moderate watering is required as the fleshy leaves store moisture; occasional liquid feeds should be diluted to half-strength. Loam-based soil balances the weight of a tall plant. The roots are best kept confined and will eventually break the pot, so repotting is rarely necessary, though the plant is long-lived.

Special note
Overwatering and cold conditions can damage this tolerant plant

| Easy to grow |
| Light position |
| Cool conditions |
| All year round |

SAXIFRAGA

MOTHER OF THOUSANDS

The common name refers to the many plantlets that will hang from the parent on fine red stems. Saxifraga's leaves are deep green veined with silver, with red-purple undersides. The plant is best displayed in a hanging basket or on a high shelf; it grows only about 23cm (9in) high, but the trailing 'babies' are a delightful feature. Saxifraga is kept as a foliage plant, though small white flowers on fine stems may appear in late summer.

Provide a light, cool environment; some mild sun every day encourages growth. In temperatures higher than 16°C (60°F) increase humidity around the pot. Water the compost thoroughly from spring to autumn, sparingly in winter. Pot on in spring, in a loam-based compost. To propagate, detach larger plantlets and root them separately. These can replace an ageing parent plant, which may become straggly and unkempt after three or four years.

Special note
Keep a careful eye out for insect pests; the plant is most vulnerable if conditions are too warm and dry

| Easy to grow |
| Light position |
| Cool conditions |
| All year round |

SCHEFFLERA

UMBRELLA TREE

This plant is named the Umbrella Tree for the way the elongated, glossy leaflets radiate from the stems. It is branching when young, though with a strong central stem, but as it ages it does develop a tree-like habit; lower leaves fall and the 'trunk' thickens. It is slow-growing but will eventually reach at least 1·8m (6ft), even in a pot, and can grow up to 3m (10ft) indoors.

High humidity is very important. Double-pot with a layer of moist peat, and spray leaves frequently with tepid water. Provide an evenly warm temperature – ideally, not above 21°C (70°F) and not below 13°C (55°F). Schefflera prefers good light; it will adapt to partial shade but does not grow so well. Keep compost moist and feed regularly during active growth. Pot in a gritty, loamy compost, moving the plant to a larger pot every second year.

Special note
If the central growing point of a large plant is pruned, it cannot resume fresh growth and will remain stubby

| Easy to grow |
| Light position |
| Warmth and moisture |
| All year round |

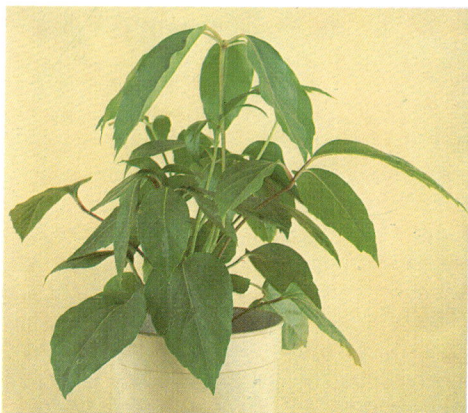

SCHLUMBERGERA

EASTER CACTUS

The Easter Cactus is S. *gaertneri*, a spreading plant up to 60cm (2ft) high, with fleshy, scalloped stems and bright scarlet trumpet-shaped flowers appearing in late spring.

Water the plant generously while it is in flower and give a monthly feed through spring and summer. Provide a bright, warm position as long as the flowers last. In summer the plant can stand outdoors in a warm, slightly shaded spot. Bring it indoors in autumn and allow a rest period, keeping it cool and barely moist in subdued light. In late winter gradually increase watering and as flower buds appear, resume full care. Schlumbergera can be repotted annually after flowering, in a soil and sand mixture. Detached stem sections will root in a mixture of peat and sand. Take cuttings from the upper stems in spring and allow them to dry out for two or three days before potting them up.

Special note
Do not move the
plant around once
flower buds have set,
or they will fall

| Easy to grow |
| Light position |
| Warm conditions |
| Flowers in spring |

SCINDAPSUS

DEVIL'S IVY

In the wild this climbing plant will attach itself to tree trunks, using strong aerial roots. Indoors, it can be treated as a climber or trailer. The tough, shiny, heart-shaped leaves of S. *aureus* are marked with gold. It is the easiest plant of this genus to grow. The more brightly marked cultivar 'Marble Queen' and the grey-green species S. *pictus* need more warmth and light.

S. *aureus* retains its markings in poor light and will adapt to a light or shaded position. Give it a warm and humid environment, winter minimum 10°C (50°F). Keep the compost thoroughly watered from spring to autumn, barely moist in winter. Feed young plants weekly, more established specimens every two or three weeks, during active growth only. Pot on each spring, in soil-based compost, up to a 20cm (8in) pot, then top-dress the compost annually. Stem cuttings taken in spring should be set four or five to a pot.

Special note
Cut back main stems
at the start of a new
growing season to keep
the plant in good shape

| Easy to grow |
| Light or partial shade |
| Warmth and moisture |
| All year round |

SEAFORTHIA LUTESCENS

SEAFORTHIA PALM

This palm has a broad spread, since each heavily ribbed frond grows to a length of 1·3m (4ft) and is at least 60cm (2ft) across, but it is slow-growing. The fronds arch out from clustered stems; their colouring is yellow-green and the plant is also described by the common name of Golden Feather Palm.

In common with other palms, this plant can tolerate or even thrive in low light, but the foliage grows most strongly in bright, warm and humid conditions. However, it should be screened from direct sun or placed just away from a sunny window. Keep the compost moist at all times if the room is constantly warm, and spray the leaves; reduce watering if the temperature falls to the minimum 13°C (55°F). Feed an actively growing plant every two weeks. Pot on every second year in loam-based compost and keep it packed firmly around the strong base of the plant.

Special note
If the rootball is allowed to dry out the fronds harden and turn completely yellow

| Easy to grow |
| Light position |
| Warmth and moisture |
| All year round |

SENECIO CRUENTIS

CINERARIA

This is a temporary houseplant, flowering in late winter or early spring. It can be quite tall, depending upon variety, from 30cm (12in) to 60cm (2ft). The spreading leaves are heart-shaped, toothed and bright green. Clustered flower heads consist of daisy-shaped flowers with yellow or red centres and white, pink, red, orange, red-purple or blue-purple petals. These often shade towards white at the centre of the flower.

Keep Cineraria cool and moist, in an airy, well-lit position, but not under the heat of the midday sun. Water generously and evenly throughout the flowering period. If roots are allowed to dry the plant will collapse, and even when revived, its active life is shortened. No repotting is necessary as it is a temporary plant, but it will benefit from a fortnightly feed.

Special note
Look out for aphids
and whitefly, which
can attack flower buds
and young leaves

| Easy to grow |
| Light position |
| Cool conditions |
| Winter and spring |

SINNINGIA

FLORIST'S GLOXINIA

There are many different species and varieties of Sinningia, but the one commonly sold as Gloxinia is *S. speciosa*. This has a rosette of soft, oval leaves, mid-green with lighter veining, and the flowers, which appear in July, are flaring trumpet-shaped blooms on separate stalks rising just above the leaves. The height and spread of each plant is between 23cm (9in) and 30cm (12in).

The plants grow from tubers and become completely dormant in winter. While flowering they require good light – though direct sun is not necessary – and warm, humid conditions. Water generously and feed regularly during this period. Gradually reduce watering as leaves fade, remove top growth and store the tuber dry for six to eight weeks. Repot it in peaty compost in early spring, keep it warm and gradually resume watering. It will only survive three flowering seasons and should then be discarded.

Special note
Provide a humid
atmosphere but do not
spray leaves or flowers
directly

| Needs extra care |
| Light position |
| Warmth and moisture |
| Flowers late summer |

SOLANUM

WINTER CHERRY

This is a bushy shrub growing up to 38cm (15in) in both height and spread. The dark green, lance-shaped leaves are slightly toothed and undulating. Small white flowers appear in summer and are followed by berries that are green at first but in late autumn gradually turn through yellow to orange or red. The fruits are not edible: *Solanum* is the Nightshade genus. The plants are treated as annuals or kept on for only one more fruiting season.

Solanum benefits from a cool, airy position. It can be placed outdoors in summer, shielded from hot, direct sun. If it must live in a warm room, provide a moist environment and spray the leaves. Water generously in spring and summer to keep the compost thoroughly damp. If keeping the plant for a second season, reduce watering to create a six-week rest period in early spring, then repot in a soil compost and prune back the growth severely.

Special note
Spray the plant often with tepid water during flowering; this helps to set the fruits

| Easy to grow |
| Light position |
| Cool conditions |
| Fruits autumn/winter |

SPARMANNIA

INDOOR LIME

This is a vigorous, spreading shrub with attractively fresh, lime-green foliage. Its central stem is green and straight when young, becoming branching and woody as it ages. Each leaf is broadly heart-shaped, tapering to a fine point. A mature plant may produce flowers in late winter or early spring – clusters of small white blooms with prominent golden centres.

Allow the plant mild winter sun to encourage flower buds; give it a bright but sunless position in summer. A steady, moderate temperature is preferable. Roots grow rapidly and must be kept moist in spring and summer, though less so in winter. Feed the plant every two weeks during active growth, weekly if it is producing a lot of new leaves. Pot on in loam-based compost when roots fill the pot, which may be more than once a year for a young plant. Stem cuttings root easily.

Special note
Pinch out the central growing tip of a young plant to encourage branching; prune back older plants quite severely in spring

| Easy to grow |
| Light position |
| Moderate conditions |
| All year round |

SPATHIPHYLLUM

PEACE LILY

S. wallisii grows about 30cm (12in) high; the cultivar 'Mauna Loa' attains about twice that size. Both have lance-shaped, glossy leaves borne on separate stalks growing directly from a rhizome. The flower is a broad white spathe surrounding a long white or creamy spadix. It lasts about two months, gradually turning green.

In summer the plant should be placed in bright filtered or indirect light, but it can stand mild sun in winter. An even temperature of 18°C (65°F) all year round is ideal; the plant rests if it is too cold or too warm. Keep up high humidity and spray leaves frequently in the warmer months. Always allow the top layer of compost to dry out between waterings and feed the plant occasionally throughout the year. Pot on annually, in loam or peat mixture, up to a 20cm (8in) pot size. To propagate, divide the rhizome base, taking sections with two or three leaves attached.

Special note
When the flower has faded remove the whole stalk, not just the spathe

| Easy to grow |
| Light position |
| Warm conditions |
| Spring and summer |

STREPTOCARPUS

CAPE PRIMROSE

This genus now includes many different hybrids, with coarse, bright green leaves growing in a rosette arrangement from which flower stems emerge to bear single or clustered, trumpet-shaped blooms. These may be white, pink, red, purple or the blue tone of the original plant. The largest plants are 30cm (12in) tall.

Streptocarpus can flower from spring to autumn, given bright light shielded from direct sun, and a warm, moist environment. It cannot tolerate cold, and rests if the temperature drops below 13°C (55°F). Keep up humidity around the pot but do not spray the leaves directly. Water moderately in summer and supply half-strength feeds every two weeks. Reduce watering in winter. Pot on the plant each spring in a coarse peat potting mixture. It prefers a shallow pot, maximum width 15cm (6in). Divide large plants at repotting time or take leaf section cuttings.

Special note
A position close to fluorescent light at night will help to prolong flowering

| Easy to grow |
| Light position |
| Warm conditions |
| Spring to autumn |

TRADESCANTIA

WANDERING SAILOR

These popular trailing plants have small, oval leaves growing directly from the stems. The most commonly sold types have green leaves striped with white, some with purple undersides or tending to take on a pink tinge in bright light. The trailing stems can grow very long, but become bare and straggly with age. Tiny flowers may appear, but each lasts only one day.

The plant will tolerate some shade, but leaf growth and colouring are richest in bright light and fairly humid warmth. It dislikes hot, dry air from central heating appliances. Water generously from spring to autumn, giving frequent weak feeds. In winter just moisten the compost and make sure it never dries out completely. Maintain the plant in a small pot, in loam-based compost. Cuttings root easily at any time during active growth and should be set four or five to a pot.

Special note
Pinch out tips to
encourage bushiness
and remove faded
leaves from the base
of stems

| Easy to grow |
| Light position |
| Moderate conditions |
| All year round |

VINCA ROSEA

MADAGASCAR PERIWINKLE

This is a small, upright shrub with glossy, dark green leaves, ellip-
tical in shape. It reaches a height of about 35cm (14in). Flowers,
in summer or autumn, are deep pink or white with rose-pink
centres. It is a perennial, but often treated as an annual, as older
plants flower less freely.

Provide a well-ventilated position with good light and some sun
every day. *Vinca rosea* lives happily in normal room temperatures,
with a night-time minimum of 12°C (50°F). Water the plant
freely from spring through to autumn and feed it fortnightly. It
may need potting on more than once in a season, but only up to a
12·5cm (5in) pot. Use a loamy soil with good drainage. Stem
cuttings can be taken in spring or early summer.

Special note
For a fine display put
several plants together
in a small tub

| Easy to grow |
| Light position |
| Warm conditions |
| Summer and autumn |

VRIESIA

FLAMING SWORD

There are several varieties of this elegant bromeliad, one most commonly available being V. *splendens*, which has smooth, strap-like leaves banded in green and brownish-purple. These grow up to 30cm (12in) long, in an arching rosette around a central cup. In a mature plant several years old, a flower spike emerges from the cup, growing tall and straight, with bright red bracts.

Give Vriesea a bright position, filtering the sun's hottest rays. Warmth and high humidity are required; mist the leaves occasionally. Pot in a peat-based compost, mixed with coarse leaf-mould. It needs repotting only every two to three years, to a maximum pot size of 12·5cm (5in). Keep the compost moist and the central cup filled with water. Give half-strength liquid feeds monthly. Offsets from the base of the plant can be detached and potted up when 7·5cm (3in) high, and must be kept warm.

Special note
Collect fresh rainwater
to supply the plant's
central cup

Needs extra care
Light position
Warm conditions
Foliage all year

YUCCA

BAYONET PLANT

Y. *aloifolia* lives up to its name of Bayonet Plant; the leaves, which sprout in clusters from the top of a fat, woody stem, have rather viciously pointed tips. They are a dark blue-green, but cultivars are also avaiable with yellow-bordered leaves or green, white and yellow stripes. Though the plant is slow-growing, the stem alone may eventually reach a height of 1·3m (4ft).

The most important requirement is bright light and some sun every day during active growth. Yucca tolerates a cool or warm environment and a dry atmosphere. Water regularly from spring to autumn and give fortnightly feeds. The compost should be barely moistened in winter. Soil potting mixture provides nourishment and its weight balances the top-heavy growth of the plant. Pot on only when roots have filled the container, up to a pot size of 30 or 38cm (12 or 15 in) and top-dress the soil in following years.

Special note
The plant will benefit from being placed out of doors in summer, with two or three hours of sun each day

| Easy to grow |
| Bright position |
| Moderate conditions |
| All year round |

ZYGOCACTUS

CHRISTMAS CACTUS

This spectacular plant has flattened, toothed stems and can reach a height of 60cm (2ft) with a broad spread. In early winter the stem tips erupt with trumpet-shaped blooms, in a deep cerise-pink or pinkish-purple. White or orange varieties may also be available.

Allow the plant a definite cycle of activity and rest. While it flowers, water it well and give it a warm, bright position. Reduce watering as the flowers fade, repot in two parts soil to one part sand and keep barely moist until spring; then resume watering, feed occasionally and put it outdoors in a sheltered place. Bring it inside again in autumn. Tip sections from the stems can be rooted in summer in a mixture of peat and sand.

Special note
Keep up humidity by misting the stems frequently

| Easy to grow |
| Light position |
| Warm conditions |
| Flowers in winter |

INDEX OF COMMON NAMES